SPELL CRAFT

FOR A MAGICAL YEAR

SARAH BARTLETT

SPELL CRAFT

FOR A MAGICAL YEAR

RITUALS AND ENCHANTMENTS FOR PROSPERITY, POWER, AND FORTUNE

FAIR WINDS

Brimming with creative inspiration, how-to projects, and useful information to enrich your everyday life, Quarto Knows is a favorite destination for those pursuing their interests and passions. Visit our site and dig deeper with our books into your area of interest: Quarto Creates, Quarto Cooks, Quarto Homes, Quarto Lives, Quarto Drives, Quarto Explores, Quarto Gifts, or Quarto Kids.

© 2015 Fair Winds Press

First published in 2015 by
Fair Winds Press, an imprint of
The Quarto Group
100 Cummings Center
Suite 265-D
Beverly, MA 01915, USA
Telephone: (978) 282-9590
Fax: (978) 283-2742
QuartoKnows.com

Fair Winds Press titles are also available at discount for retail, wholesale, promotional, and bulk purchase. For details, contact the Special Sales Manager by email at specialsales@quarto.com or by mail at The Quarto Group, Attn: Special Sales Manager, 401 Second Avenue North, Suite 310, Minneapolis, MN 55401, USA.

19 18 17 16 15   1 2 3 4 5

ISBN: 978- 1-59233-680-7

Digital edition published in 2015
eISBN: 978-1-62788-297-2

Library of Congress Cataloging-in-Publication Data available

Cover and book design by Paul Burgess at Burge Agency

Illustrations by Mike Wanke

Printed in USA

TO JESS

CONTENTS

INTRODUCTION

 hen I was in my early twenties, I worked in London and would spend my lunch hours indulging in one of my favorite pastimes: browsing the dusty shelves of antiquarian bookshops. One warm day in June, my fingers ran across a thin, leather-bound volume with no title; inside, the frontispiece read, *Invocations for the Summer Solstice*. The twenty-four thick parchment pages revealed twelve magic spells to be performed for each hour of the day between dawn and dusk. One spell stood out for me, a spell to get back a lover. (Yes, I'd recently been dumped.) I bought the book.

As the solstice was only four days away, I was tempted to try out the spell the next day. What did a few days' difference matter? Yet scrawled in

black ink in the back of the book were the words, *Invoke the right power on the right day, and only then will you have your way*. Impatient as I was to have a go at my chosen spell, I humbly waited for the twenty-first of June and the hour that was set for the spell—3 p.m.

I followed the magic recipe, used the right ingredients, and believed—oh, how I believed that my ex would come running back to me! But an hour or so after I had cast the spell, I felt disillusioned and thought it was just a silly game. Yet two weeks later, my ex phoned to say he'd made a terrible mistake, and could we meet up? Two weeks after that he moved into my flat, and a year later we got married. In fact, that fragile book was not only the trigger for my new life direction as an astrologer practicing the magical arts, but it is the inspiration behind writing this spell book for you.

So why did the spell work? At first I thought it was just luck or chance. But as I began to work more and more with astrology and magic, I realized that the specific time when certain planets, the sun, and the moon were in certain places in the heavens was related to specific auspicious times to cast specific spells. I saw this written in ancient texts, from the ancient Egyptian magi to late Renaissance astrologers, who performed a certain spell at the "right moment"— according to the position of the planets to draw on the power of the planets or gods—to help them achieve their goals.

If we align ourselves with the cycles and rhythms of the universe, just as we instinctively do to night and day, we can also help to make magic happen in our lives and have some control over our own destiny. Most of us

are awake during the day, and most of us go to sleep at night, based on our biorhythms. The sun and moon are, by correspondence, similarly associated with day and night. They also appear to have both a physical and supernatural influence upon us. It is these solar and lunar influences, plus planetary ones, that were the basis for many of the pagan and traditional festive dates throughout the year. These include days such as Wiccan Sabbats, equinoxes, and the summer and winter solstices, or days devoted to pagan deities such as the Greek goddess Aphrodite, the Hindu Gauri, or the Norse Frigga, who by virtue of their associations with the stars, were called upon for their beneficial influences.

We all want to lead a magical life—one in which we are able to both shape and take responsibility for our destinies. This book reveals how, by simply casting spells that align with the cycles of nature and the universe, you too can begin to manifest your dreams.

We begin our magic by understanding how the natural world is aligned with the magical world, whether by correspondences, associated deities, herbs, colors, the four elements, or the heavenly bodies. The first chapter describes the use of important magic tools such as the wand, athame, and cauldron. There is also a practical explanation of how to cast a magic circle of protection and how to draw a pentagram. I have also included a unique list of secret symbols used in

Renaissance magic. These talismans are used in some spells to draw on the power of specific energies.

The remaining chapters cover each month, from January to December, for any year. You can pick up the book at whatever time of year to find spells that will align you directly with the "right day," so you can have your way.

Like me, you too can create magic in your life by working with the cycles of nature to help shape your own future. Go out and be united with the stars to help bring you the magical happiness you are seeking.

And finally, to every witch reading this book, let the light of the universe shine through you every day.

Chapter 1

THE POWER OF NATURE AND MAGICAL CYCLES

WHEN YOU THINK ABOUT IT, LIFE ON EARTH CAME INTO BEING SIMPLY BECAUSE OF OUR PROXIMITY TO THE SUN. AS THE CENTER OF OUR PLANETARY SYSTEM, THE SUN'S SOURCE OF POWER HAS A DIRECT INFLUENCE ON BOTH THE WORLD AROUND US AND THE FORCE THAT PERMEATES ALL THINGS: MAGICAL POWER. IN FACT, ALL OF NATURE IS IMBUED WITH SOLAR ENERGY, WHICH IS WHY MOST OF THE MATERIALS USED FOR SPELL WORK INCLUDE CRYSTALS, PAPER, FLOWERS, HERBS, AND SO ON.

 till, it was only five hundred years ago that most of humanity believed the Earth was the center of the universe and the sun and planets revolved around it. In the sixteenth century, Polish astrologer Nicolaus Copernicus revived an ancient Greek theory that the Earth rotated daily on its axis and circled the sun. Yet even though astronomers such as Kepler and Galileo knew this theory to be true a century later, the Roman Catholic Church considered it heretical, and it wasn't until the middle of the eighteenth century that it was finally "proved" by science. All these astronomers, or rather astrologers, also believed that there was more to heaven and earth than imagined, a force that permeated and shaped the universe.

This magical force included an established system of correspondences rooted in ancient Egyptian and Greek magical texts, such as the Egyptian Papyrus of Ani (ca. 1250 BCE)

and the so-called Greek Magical Papyri—a collection of fragments of parchment from Greco-Roman spell books and magical writings dating from the second century BCE. Correspondences—that is, colors, deities, planets, talismans, plants, herbs, directions, animals, weather patterns, and so on—were all symbolic of one another. Whether sun, rain, earthquake, storm, or volcano, or even an abstract concept such as jealousy, each was identified with a presiding deity or spirit. These gods were associated with the planets, and their corresponding attributes were used in magic potions or worn as talismans to invoke their specific powers. For example, Venus is the closest planet to Earth, and it is associated with love, women, fertility, vanity, and beauty. To the ancients, Venus appeared as both the morning star and the evening star, so it was also thought at times to usher in the dawn, and at others the dusk— as ambivalent as the goddess Venus was thought to be. Going back even

further, in Paleolithic times, plants and animals were used to heal, cure, or protect; the use of symbols carved into stone or in cave paintings called on spirits or the otherworld to aid in hunting or fertility, and the natural world and its cycles were respected and honored.

In fact, magic developed from simply a means to get "help" from the powers that be, to an ability to manipulate the energy of the cosmos so that you, the individual, could control your own destiny. By working with talismans, symbols, and correspondences you could also invoke the power of the divine to see into the future, or to make changes in the world. By drawing on the sun's power and magnifying it in your life by using talismans of the solar gods and their associated correspondences—by wearing gold jewelry, lighting candles, and so on—you could keep the power of the sun on your side, ready to help you in your quest.

THE SOLAR CYCLE

Over the course of a year, as the sun appears to move through the sky along an imaginary pathway known as the ecliptic, it crosses the made-up divisions of celestial longitude, which divide the sky into twelve 30-degree slices of a circle (to make up 360 degrees). In astrology, these twelve sectors were named after the constellations—Aries, Taurus, Gemini, Cancer, Leo, Virgo, Libra, Scorpio, Sagittarius, Capricorn, Aquarius, and Pisces—and are known collectively as the zodiac, a system originally developed by Babylonian astronomers in the seventh century BCE. Strangely, as the sun "moves" through these areas, a different energy can be felt, as if the sun, planets, and their alignment to Earth create a different atmosphere throughout the year. This is one of the reasons why people born under a certain zodiac sign are said to be influenced by the qualities of that sign. For example, the sign of Aries, ruled by the planet Mars, is associated with fire, impulse, self-concern, and aggressive energy, as well as the first growth of spring, virility, and an outgoing nature. When the sun moves through the next sign, Taurus, it is ruled by Venus, and so the solar energy is associated with femininity, sexual pleasure, and indulgence.

The sun gives life. It permeates us all at some level, whether physical or spiritual. By working with this solar energy, and by harnessing the power of specific deities and their correspondences who resonate to the solar period, you can work throughout the year to help manifest your desires.

THE LUNAR CYCLE

Another important cycle in the calendar year is that of the moon, which is also shrouded in magical association. Thought to be the territory of magic and sorcery goddesses such as Hecate and Selene, it has its own unique energy, especially when full—when "lunatics" appeared to be under the moon's spell, its strange nocturnal light was associated with werewolves, dark powers, and evil. But the moon also symbolizes regrowth and spiritual truth, new beginnings, romance, art, and the beauty of silver. Many religions, such as Hinduism, still base their year on the varying lunar phases.

The moon has four phases lasting approximately 29.5 days total. These phases are the new moon, best for beginning new projects; the waxing moon, between the new moon and full moon, best for spells concerning growth and creativity; the full moon, the perfect night for fulfilling spell work, when witches celebrate the "esbat" in honor of the moon goddess; and the waning moon, between full moon and dark new moon, best for slowing down, finishing off projects, and casting spells for banishing or releasing energy.

SEASONAL CYCLES AND FESTIVITIES

No matter where you live, the seasons change—in some places more dramatically than others. This is dependent on the tilt of the Earth and its relationship to the sun. In ancient times, weather was held responsible for life or death, fertility and growth, the harvest and the dormant season. In many traditions, the deities associated with the weather, were invoked to increase or diminish their seasonal power. Similarly, you can use magic to tap into the power of the seasons and their gods to invoke the right energy for improving your own life and journey. You can work with these energies at any time of year, but by using them at the allotted period, you increase your chances of success tenfold.

It was often because of the seasonal, planetary, or universal energy changes that worldwide cultures held traditional festivities marking these changes, such as the time for harvest, the fertility rites of springtime, the Chinese New Year, the Roman festival of Cybele, and so on. Just as you can hone your spell casting with the seasons by harnessing the power of these important moments and dates, and using ingredients and rituals associated with these times, you will be in harmony with the goals or destiny you envisage for yourself.

MAGIC TOOLS

Working within the seasons and celestial cycles is only part of successful spell work. A few magic tools are also an essential part of a witch's stock. However, you don't have to buy any of these; they can all be found at home, or used in a symbolic way. A wand can be your favorite pen; an athame, a kitchen knife; a chalice, a pretty cup; or a cauldron, your aluminum pan.

ALTAR

It isn't always possible to have a permanent altar in your home. You can perform most of the spells in this book on a table, but if you can, create a sacred space or corner of a room— even if it's just a window ledge. You'll then be ready to practice creative rituals and spells in your special place.

Altars usually consist of a flat surface, covered with cloth. A pair of candlesticks, a picture of your favorite deity, and a selection of crystals or magic charms that mean something personally to you can be placed on the altar at the back, with enough room at the front for casting spells.

WAND

The wand is symbolic of the element Air and is used to point to the spirits of the four directions or to cast a protective circle around you. It can be made from a stick, twig, or even a roll of paper. Be creative and carve your stick with symbols, such as glyphs or runes, or words sacred to you.

ATHAME

An athame is a ceremonial dagger, with a double-edged blade and usually a black handle. It is associated with the element Fire and is often used as a ritualistic tool for pointing at magical ingredients when saying a charm and directing and channeling psychic energy.

CHALICE

A chalice is simply a goblet-shaped container. Associated with the element Water, it is often filled with magical ingredients before a spell is cast. The base is symbolic of the material world, the stem of the connection between man and spirit, and the opening of receiving spiritual energy.

CAULDRON

Cauldrons are simple cooking pots. They are used to combine magical ingredients or as a receptacle for burning away petitions written on paper, once a spell has been set. Representing the element Earth, they symbolize not only the goddess but also the womb.

CANDLES

Most of the spells in this book use candles. They can be any you particularly like, whether votives, tapers, or tea lights, unless a type is specifically mentioned in the ingredient list.

MAGIC TIPS

Many of the spells in this book use simple ingredients such as candles, pen and paper, and a range of symbols, but there are also a few important symbolic components that you should learn to help protect you from negative energy, and to strengthen your contact with the magical world.

DRAWING A PENTAGRAM

Pentagrams are often drawn at the beginning of or during a spell-casting session, as they act as a protective element against any unwanted negativity. The pentagram is associated with all the elements, and the points represent Earth, Air, Fire, Water, and Spirit. Sometimes it also symbolizes love, wisdom, knowledge, law, and power. The Wiccan pentagram is drawn "upright," with the single point on top. This differs from the Satanic, or inverted, pentagram, which has its single point at the bottom.

A magic pentagram is drawn in one line without taking your pen off the paper. This imbues it with magical power, as it is thought that one complete line, like drawing a circle, represents the universe. Once you know how to draw a pentagram, you

can also use it as a symbol of power and protection by drawing it in the air before any spell craft.

With a pen,
1. Start at the lower left point of the star.
2. Draw a slightly angled line up to start the top point.
3. Draw a slightly angled line down to mark the bottom right point.
4. Draw diagonally across to make the top left point.
5. Cross horizontally straight across to mark the top right point.
6. Draw diagonally back down to meet the bottom left point you started from.

HOW TO CAST THE MAGIC CIRCLE

Magic circles are often used for more complex work because they protect you from a wide variety of unwanted energies, which can get in the way of your spell. Magic circles are best done outside, because you are then drawing directly on the electromagnetic forces of the landscape. You can first practice this at home, but it puts you directly in touch with the magic in nature if you can do it outside. Choose a quiet place, perhaps your garden, in the countryside, in a park, or even on a beach. Take a compass if you aren't very good at working out which direction you are facing!

Facing east, stand upright, extend your right hand, and point your index finger to the ground. As you slowly

pivot around, draw an imaginary circle around you on the ground in a clockwise direction until you arrive at the east again. As you draw the imaginary circle, repeat the following:

"I draw this magic circle for protection and to show I am at one with the heavens and the spirits of the four directions."

Next, you have to call in the spirits. With your right hand outstretched again, point your finger to the east and call in the east spirit.

Say,

"I call you, spirit of the East, to help me be touched with inspiration and innovative ideas."

Repeat this charm in each of the other three directions, doing so in a clockwise direction: from the east, call in the spirit of the south, then the west, and finally the north.

Now that you have called in the spirits, stand quietly for a moment in the center of your magic circle and quietly prepare yourself for the next stage of whatever spell you are working with.

GEOMANCY

The practice of geomancy originated with ancient Middle Eastern shamans who drew mystical patterns in the sand to invoke earth energies. In medieval Europe, the famous magician and astrologer Cornelius Agrippa developed sixteen mystical symbols from these ancient shamanic patterns. Similar to the Taoist oracle, the I Ching, Agrippa's geomancy symbols correspond to the astrological elements, planets, and their associated crystals. Throughout this book, you will be using crystals and these symbols together.

By tapping into the earth's invisible electromagnetic energy—the silent magic of the earth—via the vibration of crystals and their associated power symbols, you can use this energy to harness what you truly want.

The Greater Fortune	The Lesser Fortune	Solis
Via	Populus	Lunae
Acquisitio	Laetitia	Jovis
Puella	Amissio	Veneris
Conjunctio	Albus	Mercurii
Puer	Rubeus	Martis
Carcer	Tristitia	Saturni
Dragons Head	Dragons Taile	The Nodes

HOW TO BE A GOOD WITCH

Spell work first begins with your own moral responsibility when performing magic. When you perform any magic spell or enchantment, you must be honest with yourself and accept that you are doing it not only for the good of yourself, but also for everyone else. "What goes around comes around," according to the law of witchcraft, and ill intentions sent out may be visited upon you—usually threefold. So remember, never cast spells in a moment's impulse, in anger, or to hurt or upset others. Each time you cast a spell, think about your motives: Are they with goodwill, with no intentions of hurting anyone else?

Every time you work with the magical world, accept that there are unseen powers that may be difficult to contact. This is why performing spells at certain times of year creates the right interface between you, the spell, and the magical powers of the heavens. As witches, we must respect the workings of the universe and its magic, and it may be that at times we simply didn't quite get it right. (Perhaps we just didn't believe in the magic enough for it to work.) What you must never do is worry or dwell on spells that don't work. Rather, move on, try again, and most of all find deep within yourself a real sense of belief. The next time, you will succeed.

When casting spells, you must truly believe in the magic of the universe. You must truly believe that what you are doing is going to work and that you're going to make something beneficial happen. Once you have accepted this, you will be quickly on your way to creating spells that will help you to form your own destiny, just as you want it to be.

Chapter 2

JANUARY

Spells and Enchantments for Prosperous Living

Theme:
New Beginnings

Plant Energy:
Camellia for Creativity

Crystal Power:
Garnet for Prosperity

FOR MOST OF US, JANUARY IS A MONTH FOR CELEBRATION, FUN, AND RESOLUTIONS TO CHANGE OUR WAYS FOR THE BETTER. NAMED AFTER JANUS, THE ROMAN GOD OF THRESHOLDS AND DOORWAYS, JANUARY REMINDS US THAT AS ONE DOOR CLOSES, ANOTHER ONE OPENS.

ccording to Roman mythology, Janus was a god whose magical powers resided in his ability to see the future and the past simultaneously. Usually depicted with two faces, Janus was also the god of new beginnings, and so the first month of the year was named after him.

The earliest Roman calendar was made up of ten months totaling 304 days. But around 713 BCE, the king of Rome, Numa Pompilius, is supposed to have added the months of January and February so that the calendar was equivalent to a lunar year of 354 days. Similarly, in Chinese and other Eastern traditions, New Year's Day falls on a variable date during the last two weeks of January and the first two weeks of February, based on a lunar calendar.

The first day of the Roman calendar year became auspicious for casting magic for a prosperous future, and it was customary to exchange good wishes, as well as to give dates, figs, and honey as tokens of well-being. Cakes made of spelt (a kind of wheat flour) and salt were offered to Janus and burned on sacred altars.

Janus is also thought to be the male equivalent of the Roman goddess Diana, once known as Jana. In Italy, the old medieval witchcraft religion known as *Stregheria* worshipped Diana as queen of the wise women healers. She was associated with woods, mountains, and moonlight on a winter's night.

In the northern hemisphere, the sun, now past the shortest day of the winter solstice, gives us about four more minutes of daylight every day. In the southern hemisphere, the sun is slowly providing fewer daylight hours. As such, this month's spell work is all about focusing on enterprising projects while sustaining positive self-belief in your own success. With the sun moving from determined Capricorn to innovative Aquarius around the 20th, the energy and theme throughout January is about new beginnings, new ideas, positive wishes for the year ahead, and prosperity. The energy is ripe for casting spells and enchantments that will secure progress in your goals for financial growth, prosperity, or success.

January |

JANUS AND DIANA'S FESTIVAL

ENCHANTMENT FOR OPENING THE DOORWAY TO PROSPERITY

The first day of the new year is always a time to make promises or resolve to make the year a positive and prosperous one. With the help of the Roman god of new beginnings, Janus, and the goddess Diana's influence, you can step into the new year with viable resolutions for the year ahead.

 iana was worshipped in the countryside, and gifts and offerings of fruit were left in forests or at crossroads. To invoke the power of Janus, salt and cakes were placed on a sacred altar. For this spell, you're going to combine the ingredients necessary into one special enchantment.

Place the bag of earth in the center of your altar to invoke the power of Diana's abundance. Then place the three cupcakes in front of the bag, and lastly the tiny cup of salt at the front. Now light the two candles to invoke your deities, and as you place them on either side of your offering, say or whisper the following:

WHAT YOU WILL NEED

A handful of earth taken from each of the following places and gathered in a paper bag (if you can't get to any of these places, then three handfuls of earth from your own or a friend's garden will also work):

A crossroads
A forest, woods, or park
Beside a river, stream, or lake

3 cupcakes

A tiny cup of sea salt

2 white candles

> *"Diana, Janus, hear my prayer*
> *and bless this sacred altar.*
>
> *For all year long let earth's riches*
> *empower me.*
>
> *Let abundance bring me happiness.*
>
> *Let your wholeness bring me*
> *prosperity."*

Say this three times, and then thank your deities.

> *"Thank you, Diana, for your help.*
> *Thank you, Janus, for your direction."*

Now leave the candles burning for a few minutes while you gaze at your altar and calm your mind. Later, empty the bag of earth somewhere outside where you feel really happy to be, and as you sprinkle the earth on the ground, Janus and Diana will start to work the magic of prosperous living into your life.

THE FESTIVAL OF BEFANA

A PROSPERITY SPELL TO REALIZE YOUR GOALS

The night before Epiphany is a traditional celebration throughout Italy and in folklore is associated with the appearance of the Italian witch Befana. Befana is still thought to bring gifts to children on Epiphany eve. She flies through the air on a broomstick, enters the house down the chimney, and fills socks and shoes with sweets and presents. She then sweeps the floor to clear away the problems of the year before departing on her broomstick.

With this simple spell, you can ask Befana not only to make your home a prosperous one, but to send you auspicious energy concerning your success and enterprises over the coming year.

In the evening, place your magical charms of three figs or dates or a small cup of honey (traditional offerings to Befana) on a table beside the red candle. All these ancient offerings to Befana show that you honor her powers.

Light the red candle, draw up a chair, and sit quietly for two minutes, gazing at the candle flame to still your mind and calm the energy around you. The red candle is a symbol of your own power to realize your goals, and it also calls upon the power of Befana. Now say the following out loud or in your head, three times:

Once you have repeated this spell three times, take the broom or brush and begin to sweep the broom clockwise around the room, sweeping toward a central spot to gather all Befana's beneficial energy in one place. (Leave the broom and dust overnight.)

" Come Befana, come to me
Come from the mountains to set me free
Come with your gifts of wisdom and cheer
To make this for me a most prosperous year "

Finally, blow out the candle, and as you do, thank Befana for her help:

" Thank you, Befana, for giving me the gifts of wisdom and prosperity."

The next day remove the broom, clear up any dust or debris, and look forward to a hugely prosperous year.

WHAT YOU WILL NEED

1 red candle placed on an altar or table

3 figs, 3 dates, or a small cup of honey

1 broom or brush

January 19/20

THE SUN MOVES INTO AQUARIUS

A SPELL TO BRING YOU POSITIVE, LIFE-CHANGING IDEAS

As the sun moves into Aquarius on or around this day, the time dawns to draw inspiration for a prosperous year ahead. This ancient spell will enable you to draw on the power of the planet Uranus, the astrological ruler of Aquarius.

 or this spell, you will first need to cast a magic circle around you and call in the four directions that rule the elements Earth (north), Fire (south), Air (east), and Water (west) (see page 15). The four spirits who rule the directions are also the messengers of the gods, and these spirits will bring you inspiring ideas for a prosperous year and at the same time help you fulfill your goals.

Sit cross-legged in the middle of your circle and take the white quartz crystal in your writing hand. This will enable the magical power of the planets to permeate your whole being via the vibrational energy of the crystal. Close your eyes and imagine you are holding out the crystal as an offering, and in turn the planets are sending down creative energy into your hands.

Now open your eyes and gaze at the crystal for about a minute, calmly breathing until you have stilled your mind.

With the thumb of your nonwriting hand, touch the crystal in your other hand and say,

*"By the number 1,
the spell's begun."*

Then with your second (or index) finger, touch the crystal in the opposite hand and say,

*"By the number 2,
let it be true."*

Continue with the third finger,

*"By the number 3,
so mote it be."*

With the fourth finger,

*"By the number 4,
I won't want for more."*

Finally with the fifth finger,

*"By the number 5,
the spell comes alive."*

You now need to repeat this whole number spell again five times.

When you have finished, close your eyes for a minute, breathe slowly and deeply, and close your hand around your white quartz crystal. As you do so, say,

"Thanks be to the spirits of the East, South, West, and North, and thanks to the planet Uranus for bringing new light to my life."

Place the crystal back on the ground and stand up again. Now, with your right arm outstretched and your finger pointing down, undraw your magic circle by moving slowly around counterclockwise from the east direction until you have completed one turn of the magic circle.

Place the crystal beside your bed or on your desk for five days and nights to maximize the power of this energy. Then put the crystal in a safe place for the rest of the year so the magic can do its work.

NEW YEAR'S DAY FOR TREES

A SPELL FOR POSITIVE GROWTH IN MATERIAL AFFAIRS

Tu B'Shevat, the 15th of Shevat on the Jewish calendar, is the day that marks the beginning of a "new year" for trees. This varies from year to year, but if you cast this spell on the 23rd, you will be able to tap into the energy of the midpoint between the first and last possible dates for this celebration. Many Jewish people celebrate the day of Tu B'Shevat by eating fruit mentioned in the Torah, such as grapes, figs, pomegranates, olives, and dates.

 asting this spell invokes the energy of the tree into your life. In many traditions, the oak tree is worshipped for its longevity; willows represent the ability to adapt; rowan is the tree of success. By using this spell, you will not only invite trees' positive growth but symbolically conjure their beneficial cycles throughout the year.

To align yourself with tree magic, remove three hairs from your head and tie them together with a short piece of garden twine.

Go to a wooded area, garden, or park where you won't be disturbed. Take with you the bound hairs and a much longer piece of twine.

Walk around until you find a tree you like. Some trees seem to speak to us, others seem cold and distant. But you will find that one stands out for you, simply because of its energy, look, strange shape, or stunning presence.

Tie your twined, bound hair with the longer piece of twine. Then wrap the twine around the tree trunk. As you tie it, say,

*"With hair and twine, my strength is yours, your strength is mine.
I am now bound to this sacred tree from toe to crown."*

Either place your hands on the bark of the tree or "hug" the tree literally. Rest your head against the trunk for several minutes while you relax and draw on its strength and power. Then leave your hair and twine bound around the trunk.

When you get home, draw an image of the tree on a piece of paper. Write the five words below where the points of a pentagram would fall if you were to draw it over the tree.

Wisdom

Longevity

Power

Success

Inspiration

Fold the paper up and place it in a drawer or safe place so that the power you have drawn from trees stays with you all year long.

CHINESE NEW YEAR

A FENG SHUI CHARM FOR PROSPERITY

The Chinese new year falls on a day within two weeks of this date, depending on the lunar calendar. If you perform this ancient Chinese feng shui enchantment, you can be sure that whether it's the Year of the Rat or Year of the Dragon, the energy is aligned in your home for a prosperous year ahead. Feng shui ("feng" meaning "wind" and "shui" meaning "water") is the Chinese art of placement for harmonious living. It is aligned to Taoist magic, which dates back to 2000 BCE. This use of energy alignment has also been used in acupuncture and Chinese healing arts.

In feng shui, the placement of crystals in your home corresponds to certain energies that will benefit your wealth and success. The northwest and west areas of your home correspond to success and prosperous living, while diamonds, selenite, white quartz, and silver all are symbolic of financial success.

WHAT YOU WILL NEED

1 white candle

A silver gilt or silver-framed mirror

A silver chalice, cup, or bowl (pewter or stainless steel)

A silver or silver-colored necklace

1 diamond, piece of selenite, or white quartz crystal

A red envelope, packet, or sheet of red paper folded up, containing 3 silver or silver-colored coins

First, create a sacred corner in the west or northwest corner of your home. This can be on a raised table, shelf, or window ledge. To make the area sacred, simply light a white candle and stand it in the corner. Now say,

"Welcome to the deities of heaven and earth, and to the Jade Emperor, ruler of heaven."

To empower you with self-belief and added motivation for the rest of the year, place the silver-framed mirror against the wall and the silver vessel in front of the mirror. Drape a silver necklace around the mirror. Place a diamond, piece of selenite, or white quartz crystal in front of the mirror too, and in front of those, the red envelope (red is symbolic of success in Chinese tradition). These metal totems will improve your business and career dealings and bring you the success you deserve.

Remove all the items at the end of the following month and store safely away.

NEW MOON SPELL

A CHARM FOR FINANCIAL STABILITY

As with many of the monthly new moon and full moon spells, this spell aligns with the astrological energy for the month in question but can also be performed at other new moons or full moons throughout the year.

over a small table with the silk or voile; blue is the color of the feng shui element Water, which symbolizes the West and prosperity. Hang up or lean a painting or photograph of waves at sea or a waterfall, so long as the water is "moving" (in order to keep money "flowing" in your direction).

Place the two pieces of blue agate or lapis lazuli in the small glass vessel to bring beneficial energy to all you do.

Place three stems of three-leaf clover (if you find any with four, that's even more auspicious) in the west corner of your home for three days and three nights to encourage financial stability.

Finally, carry a piece of amber to promote your positive presence in any environment.

WHAT YOU WILL NEED

A piece of silk or voile in a shade of dark blue or aquamarine

A painting or photograph of moving water

2 pieces of blue agate or lapis lazuli

A small glass vessel

3 stems of three-leaf clover

1 piece of amber

FULL MOON SPELL

ENCHANTMENT TO ATTRACT MONEY

This enchantment can help you when you really feel that you don't have enough money to get through the month. Remember not to use it for greed, but only for real need.

Fortuna was the Roman goddess of luck, both good and bad, so if you want to ensure she brings you good luck, repeat to yourself that you need

"good luck"

in your life rather than just "luck."

Just before you go to bed, braid the seven strands of natural thread together. As you do so, repeat the following:

" Sweet goddess Fortuna, of fortune and luck, Let money come to me this way Without ill intent, for this I pray."

Repeat your spell over and over as you braid the strands. Repeat again as you tie nine knots all along the braided cord. Nine is the magic number of gold and also the number that brings truth and clarity.

As you tie the knots, visualize your financial needs being met. Keep repeating the spell out loud until you have tied the nine knots.

Place the knotted cord under your bed to encourage Fortuna's good luck in money into your life.

WHAT YOU WILL NEED

7 strands of a fine natural thread, such as silk or cotton, about 1 foot (30 cm) to 2 feet (60 cm) long

CHARISMA SPELL

A GENERAL SPELL FOR ANY DAY OF THE MONTH

There are times when we just want to feel good about ourselves, to shine, to radiate, and to feel we have the charisma of a star. It is charisma, which is itself magical, and it's going to be all yours after you perform this spell.

The word *charisma* originates from an ancient Greek word meaning "divine gift." With the help of your magic ingredients and a little help from the moon goddess, Selene, you too will be filled with charisma and attraction.

Place the three candles in a triangle or pyramid shape on your altar or a table, with the white one at the top of the pyramid, the black one to the left, and the pink one to the right. Light the candles. While the candles are burning, sprinkle the rose petals into the bowl of spring water and set it on your altar. Wait for five minutes, then one by one, remove the rose petals and place them on the table. As you do so, repeat the following:

" With each petal my beauty grows
Within, without, and all about
Hair, skin, face, and inner wealth
As divine as the goddess, wild but svelte. "

Now return the rose petals to the bowl,
with a little perfume added. Anoint
the potion with a rose petal behind
your knees, inner elbows, wrists, neck,
and temples. As you do so, say,

"By the power of cosmos, moon, and sun
By the power of three be done
By the power of three, times two and three
As I will, so mote it be."

Only on the eve of the full moon, pour
the remaining mixture away. As you
do so, repeat the spell,

" Thrice I have charisma fine.
Thrice this beauty will be mine.
Thrice I shine, and thrice I win.
Both those to me whose love they'll bring. "

For the next two months, you will find
your charisma brings you the attention
or attraction factor you are seeking.

WHAT YOU WILL NEED

1 white candle

1 black candle

1 pink candle

5 rose petals

A bowl of spring water

Favorite perfume

Chapter 3

FEBRUARY

Spells and Enchantments for Lifestyle Changes

Theme:
Lifestyle Changes

Plant Energy:
Rowan Tree for Transformation

Crystal Power:
Amethyst for Inspiration

THE ROMAN MONTH OF FEBRUARY WAS NAMED AFTER THE LATIN *FEBRUUM*, WHICH MEANS "PURIFICATION." IN THE OLD ROMAN LUNAR CALENDAR, RITUAL PURIFICATION WAS ALWAYS HELD ON THE FULL MOON OF FEBRUARY. THE FESTIVAL FEBRUA, A TRADITIONAL SPRING CLEAN, WAS PROBABLY BASED ON THE CHANGING WEATHER WHEN THE FIRST RAINS HERALDED THE COMING SPRING. ACCORDING TO VARIOUS SCHOLARS, THE FEAST DAY DERIVES FROM AN ANCIENT MYSTICAL ETRUSCAN FESTIVAL CONCERNED WITH PURGING THE DEAD OF WINTER. FEBRUUS WAS ORIGINALLY AN ETRUSCAN GOD OF RICHES, DEATH, AND PURIFICATION AND WAS ASSIMILATED INTO THE ROMAN PANTHEON AS THE GOD OF THE SAME NAME TO PERSONIFY FEBRUARY.

 ebruary begins under the sign of Aquarius, which is ruled by the god Uranus and is associated with change, upheaval, and erratic, unpredictable, and controversial behavior. But as the sun crosses the cusp of Pisces around the 19th, the radical Aquarian energy dissolves in the misty waters of Neptune, who heralds great dreams, finding one's way, and acceptance of change and the cycles of life.

Neptune was the Roman god of the oceans, and as ruler of Pisces allows us, like the sea, to flow, change, and grow. Pisces is the last sign of the zodiac and the culmination of the astrological year. This is a time to prepare for change and ask the gods and the cosmos to help you find the depth of self-belief to move on or change your life for the better. Not only is there more light in the northern hemisphere, but Pisces heralds a mysterious energy, a time when we can get in touch with our deepest feelings, be inspired, and understand our dreams. We can also distinguish between which dreams can be made real and which dreams are illusions or wishful thinking.

By working with the radical energy of Aquarius, you can make better decisions and plan long-term changes. With the revealing energy of Pisces, you can be creative with your future. These spells harness the qualities and energies of February, whether from the magic of the Sabbat on the 2nd, known as Imbolc, the love enchantment of Saint Valentine's Day on the 14th, or the Blossom Festival on the 25th.

SAINT BRIGIT'S FEAST DAY

A SPELL FOR BIG CHANGES

Saint Brigit's feast day is the perfect time for making decisions, most importantly for those changes that are almost miracles. Brigit was a Christian saint and miracle worker who took over the Celtic goddess Brigit's role when pagan beliefs were suppressed by the Roman Catholic Church. Brigit was originally goddess of livestock, poetry, sacred wells and springs, and the arrival of early spring. In the early medieval period, nineteen nuns in Kildare, Ireland, tended a perpetual flame for Saint Brigit and her miraculous healing powers. If you want a miracle, use a large old key, which symbolizes the sacred key that unlocked the door to Brigit's sanctuary, to usher Brigit's powers into your life.

ight the red candle to ignite the energy of Saint Brigit and place it on your altar or table. Next, write down on the paper all the things you want to change in your life. They may be simple but difficult to manifest, such as a better job, a different home, moving abroad, leaving a difficult relationship, beginning a new life, or changing your lifestyle completely. Then write down a time line, or a date in the future you want them to be achieved. Once you have written the list, cross off any that seem totally impossible within your given time lines. Be realistic.

WHAT YOU WILL NEED

1 red candle

A piece of paper and a pen

1 large old metal key
(as large as you can find)

Finally, whittle your list down to one major change by using only one word. It may be just one word, such as *lifestyle* or *work* or *love*, but it will be a *big* word in your mind.

Write down your big word nine times (Brigit's magical number).

Next, take up the key and charge it with magic by slowly drawing it through the flame of the candle back and forth from right to left, left to right (without burning your fingers), nine times total.

This is the key to opening the door to your "big" word, so keep repeating that word as you draw the key through the flame nine times, then blow out the candle.

When the key has cooled down, place it under your pillow for nine nights to fill your life with Brigit's miracle power. The change you seek will be forthcoming within the time frame you wrote down on the paper.

February 2
IMBOLC SABBAT

A SPELL TO ACTIVATE SUCCESSFUL CHANGE

Marking a traditional midpoint day between the solstice of the dark of winter and the equinox of spring in the northern hemisphere, Imbolc occurs around February 1, depending on the changing ecliptic of the sun. Imbolc was also when Saint Brigit was said to visit the home; people left items of clothing or food outside for her to bless. They made a special cross and poppet (small, doll-like figure) of Brigit, known as a "Brideog," which they placed on an altar with flowers and magical herbs to invoke her power.

 ollow this old pagan spell to Brigit to ensure changes in your life are successfully completed. It draws on energy from the four elements, and the amber is used to remove all fear. You will need a Brigit cross, which is usually made from rushes or straw. You can draw this on paper with four parallel lines very close together for the horizontal bar of the cross, and four parallel lines very close together for the perpendicular bar of the cross.

WHAT YOU WILL NEED

A Brigit cross or drawing of one

A pouch filled with:
1 piece of amber (represents Earth)
1 seashell (represents Water)
1 sprig of vervain or mint (symbolizes Air)
Red rose petals (symbolizes Fire)

Fold the paper with the drawing of the Brigit cross into four, take your pouch, and go for a walk in the garden, countryside, or park, wherever you can be at one with nature. Find a quiet place to sit and relax.

Unfold the paper with the cross drawing on the ground and place the pouch on top of it. If you are using a real cross, place it on the ground and put the pouch alongside it. Now invoke the power of Brigit by saying,

"Thank you, Brigit, for bringing successful changes into my life for the rest of the year."

Take up the pouch and one by one remove the elemental symbols—it doesn't matter in which order—placing each on the paper or on the cross. When the four ingredients are laid out, say,

*"By the power of Brigit's delight
I now entertain the right
To be and have and hold and do
All that I want to change anew."*

Now say,

*"By the power of Brigit,
I welcome the big change
that is coming my way."*

Replace all your elements into the pouch, take up the paper or cross, and return home. Soon your dreams will unfold.

SAINT VALENTINE'S DAY

MAGIC RING AND LOVE SPELL TO CHANGE SOMEONE'S HEART

Saint Valentine was thought to be a Christian martyr who healed his jailer's daughter and, just before his execution, sent her a letter that read, "Farewell, from your Valentine." By the medieval period, the day became associated with romance among courtly lovers, and spells were cast to ensure success in love. One such beautiful seductress was Dangereuse de l'Isle Bouchard, who, in her quest to woo William, Duke of Aquitaine, called on the goddess Venus to spellbind William to her. Follow in Dangereuse's seductive footsteps and make your Valentine fall for you, too.

WHAT YOU WILL NEED

A piece of black paper and a silver pen

A simple silver or silver-colored ring or band with no markings. (It doesn't have to fit your finger, because this is one ring you won't be wearing on your hand.)

2 lengths of red silk ribbon or thread

2 bay leaves

1 willow leaf

1 rowan tree leaf (if not available, 1 piece of rose quartz)

A glass or glass bowl filled with rosewater

 agic rings have been used since medieval times to draw love to you, especially if someone hasn't noticed you or you have been rejected. These rings were often entwined with either the hair of the loved one or a red ribbon. For the spell to truly work, you must never tell that person about this talisman or it will break the spell.

First, write the name of the one whose feelings you want to change on the piece of paper with the silver pen.

Take the ring and twine the red ribbon or thread around and around it until the ring is covered. As you do so, say,

*"Thrice I bind, thrice times their love for me.
Thrice I bind and thrice times thrice their ecstasy.
For with this charm they will be mine.
Not bound, but free to love in chosen time."*

Gently drop the leaves and the ring into the bowl of rosewater. Place the paper in a window, on a ledge or table nearby, where it will be activated by the moon.

Place the bowl of water with the ring and other ingredients upon the paper. On the following evening, remove the ring from the water, wait for the ribbon to dry even if it takes a day or so, then thread the ring—still bound by the ribbon—onto another piece of silk cord. Wear it around your neck and say,

*"Thank you, Venus, for this gift.
My love will turn, the change will be,
My love will see, then love will turn,
A heart will change and come to me."*

Keep wearing the ring for three more days or keep it in a pouch and carry it with you wherever you go. The spell will invoke change in someone's heart, or someone will see you in a new and beautiful light.

THE LUPERCALIA

February 15

A SPELL TO GIVE YOU THE COURAGE TO MAKE CHANGES

The Roman Lupercalia festival was a feast in honor of Lupa, the she-wolf who suckled the infant orphans Romulus and Remus, the legendary founders of Rome. It replaced an earlier Greek secret rite, known as the Lykaia, held on the slopes of Mount Lykaion or Wolf Mountain, where adolescent boys were believed to transform into werewolves as part of their rite of passage into adulthood.

 ou're not going to transform into a werewolf—but you are going to draw on the power and courage of the she-wolf so you have the courage to completely change your lifestyle or move on from the past and create a new future for yourself.

WHAT YOU WILL NEED

1 piece of amber

6 pieces of red/orange carnelian stone

This enchantment uses symbols that harness the Lupercalia's association with creative change and the she-wolf's motif of courageous power. It uses amber to banish negativity and carnelian stone, which is the crystal of courage, fearlessness, and bold action, to transform your life. The hexagram, or six-pointed star, is a potent symbol of both the numinous universe and the manifest one. The upward point is the symbol of the element Fire, while the downward point is the symbol of the element Water. The area in the center of the hexagram is a point of balance and beauty. This is when change can come; this is where you will stand, and where the fearless wolf has the courage to reveal itself.

First, place a piece of amber in a south-facing window of your home to get rid of any negative thoughts and boost your self-confidence.

To activate the spell, place six pieces of carnelian, arranged as the points of a six-pointed star, with enough room for you to stand in the middle. Do this preferably in a garden or outside space or, if necessary, inside your home.

Every day for the next two weeks, step into the middle of the hexagram and repeat the following spell for two minutes with your eyes closed:

"I will change my life, and change will bring me all that I long for."

You will soon be able to see the change that you desire.

February 25

BLOSSOM FESTIVAL

ENCHANTMENT FOR CAREER CHANGE

Hanami, meaning "flower viewing," is a Japanese tradition of celebrating the transient beauty of the cherry and plum blossom. In ancient Japan, families would picnic or feast under the cherry blossom trees as a celebration of the spring. As a symbol of rebirth and the fleeting nature of the blossom, its magic is harnessed to enjoy future change in career and vocation.

 irst, imagine and think clearly to yourself about what kinds of things make you feel joyful.

What gives you a sense of excitement or passion?

What things do you do or have you done where you feel as if you are lost in time, when nothing else matters to you except what you are doing?

When is work no longer work, but becomes a joyful playtime?

If you have no idea, then before you cast this spell you will need to know. So explore ideas, brainstorm with friends or partners, and seek out your true vocation.

Once you know, concentrate hard on your goal while you cast this spell.

Light the candle and place the blossoms or the image of the blossoms alongside the vanilla pod and piece of tourmaline on a table.

Hold the three blossom twigs or image in your hands as you say,

" I charge this blossom to invoke a new vocation or successful career change into my life. So let it be. "

Place the twigs or photo back on the table and now hold the vanilla pod, renowned for invoking a sense of peaceful power, for a few seconds in the candle flame. Say,

" I charge this candle to invite a new vocation or a successful career change into my life. So let it be. "

Place the vanilla pod back on the table.

Lastly, take the green tourmaline, a symbol of prosperity, and say,

" I charge this crystal to ignite success in all the changes I make. So let it be. "

Let the candle burn all the way down before blowing it out and leave your offerings overnight for the blossom spell to work its magic.

NEW MOON SPELL

A SPELL FOR NEW ROMANCE

If you are looking for new romance, then this spell should be cast just after the new moon to draw on the power of Selene, the moon goddess.

lace the cauldron or cooking pot on your altar between two lit pink candles. Gently drop the essential oils into the cauldron.

Light the incense and as you do so, say,

> *"Selene, Goddess*
> *of the moon,*
> *Lady of enchanted light,*
> *let love be mine and soon."*

Next, tap the cauldron five times with your wand or silver spoon. Say,

> *"One to seek him/her,*
> *Two to find him/her,*
> *Three to bring him/her,*
> *Four to bind him/her,*
> *Heart to heart,*
> *forever one.*
> *So with Five,*
> *this spell is done."*

Tap the cauldron five more times.

Place the wand or silver spoon beside the cauldron and extinguish the candles to speed the spell upon its way.

Every evening for two weeks, repeat the words of your spell. As you do so, tap your finger five times on the rose quartz love charm you're wearing or carrying.

By the next new moon, your seductive charm will have drawn new romance to you.

WHAT YOU WILL NEED

A cauldron or cooking pot

2 pink candles

3 drops each of essential oils of
Rose
Lavender
Jasmine

Sandalwood incense

A wand or silver or silver-colored spoon

1 piece of rose quartz (either carry with you in your pocket or bag or wear as jewelry)

FULL MOON SPELL

MIRROR ENCHANTMENT TO BANISH BAD LUCK AND INVOKE GOOD LUCK

In many traditions, ranging from Chinese feng shui to traditional European witchcraft, mirrors are used to ward off the evil eye or to banish negativity.

On the day of the full moon, take with you a small vanity mirror. You may be at work, out having fun, or staying at home, but you are going to banish negative energy around you so that good luck, harmony, and happiness come your way.

Wherever you are, discreetly take the mirror in your hand and reflect all that is around you. This removes negativity and causes no harm to anyone.

When you get home, place the mirror face down in a place where no one else can pick it up or wrap it in black fabric and put it in a drawer overnight.

As you do so, say,

The next morning in daylight, take the mirror outside, hold it up to face the direction of the sun for nine seconds (the number of universal reward), and the negativity will be burned away and replaced by positive solar energy to bring you good luck.

"Planets, Earth, Air, Water, Fire
Aligned to bring my heart's desire:
Bad luck turn and bad luck flee.
Good luck and fortune comes to me."

WHAT YOU WILL NEED

Small vanity mirror

BUSINESS SUCCESS POTION

In ancient Chinese traditions, Hsi Ho was the mythical mother of the sun. She stretched out her son's golden arms every morning to revitalize the Earth and bathed the child every morning in the east-shore lake so he would shine brightly throughout the day. Like the sun-child, you need to shine. This magic potion will draw business success, useful contacts, and deluxe living into your professional life. If you use it as a room diffuser or spray it into the office, you will be like a magnet to the professional stars, shining as brightly as the sun itself.

WHAT YOU WILL NEED

An 8-ounce (235 ml) glass jar or flacon with a lid

1/4 cup (60 ml, or 2 ounces) pure spring water

1/4 cup (60 ml, or 2 ounces) rosewater

Essential oils of Bergamot
Cinnamon
Lavender
Neroli
Rose
Geranium
Rosemary
Sandalwood
Cedar

he Chinese mystics used many potions to attract wealth, wisdom, and power to the ancient dynastic families. It's not easy to find these ingredients, so this recipe is adapted to modern-day living. The ingredients may be a little expensive, but if you want to attract wealthy enterprises, or luxury influences, you need to send that quality out to the universe.

First, in the glass jar or flacon mix equal parts of spring water and rosewater. Next add, drop by drop, eight drops of each of the essential oils. Eight is an auspicious number in Chinese magic for business success. Don't worry if they don't mix in with the water, as the two invoke the power of the sun and the moon.

Put the top on the jar and shake vigorously. As you do so, say,

"By the power of the Sun, let this potion prove
Some lavish success and wealth will move
By the power of the moon, good blessings will come
Draw business dreams to me, oh power of the One."

Use a funnel to empty some of the magic formula into a spray bottle, and then spray throughout your office, home, or business premises, concentrating particularly on thresholds, entrances, and doorways. You can add it to your laundry rinse cycle (if you are not allergic to any of the ingredients) to permeate your clothes with its magical power of attracting luxury and success.

Chapter 4
MARCH
Spells and Enchantments for Manifesting Dreams

Theme:
Manifestation

Plant Energy:
Pine Tree for Good Fortune

Crystal Power:
Aquamarine to Reveal True Desires

AN OLD ENGLISH FOLK RHYME TELLS US THAT "MARS BRINGS BREEZES LOUD AND SHRILL, STIRS THE GOLDEN DAFFODIL", AND AT THIS TIME OF THE YEAR, THERE IS A DISTINCT CHANGE IN THE WEATHER. IN THE NORTHERN HEMISPHERE, PLANTS THAT HAD SEEMED DEAD OR DORMANT BURST INTO BUD, WHILE IN SOUTHERN LATITUDES, AUTUMNAL COLORS WEAVE THROUGH THE LANDSCAPE.

arch derives its name from the Latin *Martius*, the first month of the earliest Roman calendar. Named after the Roman god of war, Mars was also regarded as a guardian of agriculture and an ancestor of the Roman people through his sons Romulus and Remus.

The sun in Pisces coincides with the end of the astrological year. We have come full circle and visited all twelve signs of the zodiac, and it is said in astrological circles that within Pisces you discover every other sign.

As the equinox falls on the 21st, so the new astrological year begins with the sun moving into Aries. This is about new beginnings, a time of fresh momentum, potency, growth, fertility, and power. The solar impetus now pushes some of us to be a little more self-assured, indulgent, desirous, and confident; while for others, perhaps those born under less strong-willed signs such as Cancer, there's an energy of self-importance and rivalry around. But for everyone, this is still a brilliant time for getting your way, taking on new challenges, pushing for what you want, and doing magic for manifesting your dreams. Neptune, the ruler of Pisces, was highly promiscuous, and he had hundreds of offspring. It is his manifesting and creative power that you can draw on throughout the first few weeks of March.

Mars is the archetypal dominant male, and yet his legends were tangled in the sheets of Venus and her feminine wiles. This led to priestesses and witches combining their individual motifs and symbols to create dream potions. The last part of the month heralds the perfect time to get your future plans organized, to use magic spells so that dreams can be fulfilled, and to know which ideals can be designated to the reject pile.

The magic spells this month will not only bring to light what you want to happen in your life, but also give you the courage to do something about those desires, which is what magic is all about: desire laced with belief, action, and utter dedication to your goals. All the things you want in your life are about to happen, aided by the energy and power of the universe.

March | MATRONALIA

A SPELL TO BRING CREATIVE AND FERTILE REWARDS

The Matronalia was an ancient Roman festival celebrating the goddess Juno as protector of childbirth, motherhood, and women. In the original Roman calendar, the first of Mars was the first day of the year, when women received gifts from husbands, spells for fertility and childbirth were cast, and wealthier women gave their slaves a day off work. This Renaissance magic spell will invoke the power of fertility deities of all traditions and bring you good luck for childbirth and all issues regarding fertility and creativity, whether of the body or of the mind.

 his spell uses the symbol known as *Puella* in fifteenth-century magical geomancy (see page 16). It is made up of four large dots in a diamond shape, with a fifth dot underneath the fourth. The symbol is associated with both moonstone and rose quartz.

On the morning of the 1st, draw the Puella symbol on a piece of paper, write your name above the point at the top, and then write what you want to manifest successfully beneath the symbol. For example, you might write "pregnancy," "fertility," "good childbirth," or even "creative inspiration." Now place a piece of rose quartz on the symbol for twenty-four hours to activate the energy and to vibrate with your personal world.

After twenty-four hours, place the rose quartz under your pillow before you go to bed. Wait until a waxing moon and then place the rose quartz on the windowsill so that your fertility energy is magnified by the moon's influence. After the full moon, place it back under your pillow for two more weeks so that your female hormones, creative ideas, and childbearing ability have been imbued with this ritual energy.

Meanwhile, on the 1st, the day you started the rose quartz ritual, arrange five pieces of moonstone in the symbol of Puella, preferably outside in a safe place, with the top end of the symbol pointing toward the west. This will reinforce the rose quartz ritual and help to harness mother earth's fertility and feminine power. Within two lunar cycles, your wishes will be fulfilled. If you are pregnant and not due within these next eight weeks, repeat the spell two weeks before your due date for a happy childbirth.

WHAT YOU WILL NEED

A piece of paper and a pen

1 piece of rose quartz

5 pieces of moonstone

BACCHANALIA

A SPELL TO MAKE A WISH COME TRUE

WHAT YOU WILL NEED

A piece of paper and a pen or pencil

1 red candle

A cauldron or cooking pot

1 cup (235 ml) red wine and 1 glass of the same red wine or grape juice to drink, if you are averse to wine

The Bacchanalia consisted of various Roman festivals in honor of Bacchus, the Greco-Roman god of wine, freedom, intoxication, and ecstasy. Bacchus was the Roman equivalent of the Greek mystical god Dionysius, and both were celebrated at the beginning and end of the grape harvest. This spell uses the magic ingredients associated with both gods to manifest a special wish sooner than you think.

ake yourself comfortable and sit before your table or altar of ingredients. Think about what you want to manifest. Concentrate on it and imagine clearly what it might be like to have it. Now write down on your paper what it is you wished for.

Light the candle and focus for a few moments on the candle's flame, then take up your paper and say,

"I connect myself to the power
of Bacchus
And with this offering give
thanks.
So shall this which I have
written come to pass.
May it come to me easily,
and with harm to none.
I will it. I draw it to me.
I accept it. I receive it.
I give thanks for it.
By my will, so mote
it be."

Now place the paper in the candle flame. Hold the burning paper for as long as you safely can over the cauldron or cooking pot, then drop it in. The length of time it takes for the paper to burn is a sign of how long your wish will take to manifest. For example, if it takes only a few seconds, this corresponds to a few days, a few minutes, a few weeks, and so on. If any part of the paper doesn't burn, take that piece and repeat the spell again.

Once it has burned to cinders, pour the cup of wine over the paper cinders and say,

"I put myself into a
position of love and trust,
knowing that what
I wished for shall come."

Finally, thank Bacchus for his help by drinking the glass of wine in his honor, and then say,

"Thank you, Bacchus,
for all your help for my
future happiness."

SPRING EQUINOX

A SPELL TO MANIFEST SUCCESS

In the northern hemisphere the spring equinox has long been celebrated, because it also ushers in the first day of the astrological year—in other words, when the sun enters Aries and when night and day are approximately the same length. This change of season from winter to spring has been celebrated in many ancient cultures, where festivals were important fertility rituals to honor gods and goddesses, such as Aphrodite in ancient Cyprus, Hathor in Egypt, and Ostara in Scandinavia.

 his ancient Roman spell called on the powers of Mars and the element Fire, represented by the orange or gold candles, to create a potent mixture of positive energy to harness success.

Place the candles in a triangle shape, which enhances their ability to work with the threefold power of Mars. Don't light the candles yet, but close your eyes and relax for a few moments and then say,

"Mighty Mars,
Thank you for all that I have.
I ask you now to help me manifest success.
Aid me as I work to achieve it.
Please bring it to me when the time is right.
So mote it be."

Draw the glyph for Mars, or Martis (page 16), on the piece of paper three times in a triangle shape and place the paper in the center of the three-candle triangle.

Now, as you light each candle, say three times,

"Fire, ignite my dream for the highest good."

Concentrate on the triangle of candles for several minutes to draw on the energy and invoke the power of Mars.

Next, blow out the candles and thank Mars for his help on this equinox day.

"Thank you, Mars, for the power of success in my life."

Fold up the paper and go outside somewhere quiet and where you will be able to bury the paper in the ground or hide it beneath a large stone, boulder, or under a plant or tree. As you bury or hide it, say,

"Earth, seal my dream, for the highest good. Air, follow my dream for the greatest good. Water, nurture my dream for the highest good."

Within a few weeks, you should be in a position to manifest success.

March 25

FESTIVAL OF CYBELE

ENCHANTMENT TO FULFILL A WISH IN ONE LUNAR CYCLE

Cybele was an ancient goddess who, in Greek mythology, rejected Zeus. But while she slept, the great philanderer managed to seduce her. Eventually Cybele gave birth to Agdistis, a hermaphrodite demon so wild, the other gods feared him. In their terror, they cut off his sexual organs and from his blood sprang an almond tree.

 river nymph named Nana ate the fruit of the tree and fell pregnant; her son, Attis, was reared by shepherds. When he became a young man, his grandmother Cybele fell in love with him, but unaware, Attis fell in love with the king of Pessinus's daughter. Cybele became insanely jealous and drove Attis mad. Trying to escape her power, he ran in a craze through the mountains, stopped at the foot of a pine tree, and castrated and then killed himself. From Attis's blood

WHAT YOU WILL NEED

A handful of almonds or 3 drops of pure almond oil

A few violet flowers or 1 tablespoon (15 ml) of violet eau de toilette, perfume, or scent

A silver-colored dish

1 white candle

1 rose thorn

sprang the first violets, and Cybele, in her horror, called upon Zeus to help resurrect Attis.

The moral of this story is that we must accept that we can't always have what we want, and that even goddesses are vengeful, irresponsible, and incestuous. However, the positive magic of this enchantment draws on the strength of Cybele's power, to bring to life one wish, as she brought to life her beloved Attis.

If you use the oil and perfume method, place the almond oil first in the dish and the perfume afterward. If you use the nuts and flowers method, sprinkle the almonds onto the flowers.

Inscribe your name into the candle with a rose thorn.

Light the candle and place it beside your dish of Cybele's magic ingredients. With your eyes focused upon the flame, concentrate on your wish. When the wish is firmly in your thoughts, whisper the following words three times:

❝ Great Mountain Mother Cybele, grant my wish. Fulfill my dreams. Smile on me tonight. ❞

Extinguish the candle flame, and within the space of a lunar cycle your wish should be granted.

AHURANI

ANCIENT PERSIAN NEW YEAR

Up until the 30th of April, the ancient Persians celebrated the start of their year. Ahurani was the goddess of water, invoked at this time of year for fertility, health, peace, and wealth. It is said that she brought prosperity to the land and helped women to become pregnant. Water libations, pouring water from jars over sacred altars, were a key part of her rituals.

 n ancient Persian magic, large terra-cotta jars were used to "ferment" good energy. When the time was right, the lid would be taken off the jar and the spell would come to life. Ahurani's libation-jar spell will bring you inspiration and help you to work out exactly how to manifest your dream if you perform this ritual before the end of the day. If it's raining when you perform this ritual, so much the better; or if you are beside a lake, stream, river, or the sea, this will increase the influence tenfold.

WHAT YOU WILL NEED

7 basil leaves

7 pieces of white quartz

Spring water

A lidded jar

In a place outdoors, arrange the seven basil leaves in a circle and place the seven pieces of white quartz crystal on top of them.

Kneel or sit comfortably beside your magic circle and then, starting from the east, sprinkle a little of the spring water on each mound of crystal and basil, in a counterclockwise direction.

Place the crystals and basil leaves into the jar with the remaining water. Close the lid and either take it to a safe place in your home, perhaps under your bed where it won't be disturbed, or leave it outside in a secret place.

Three days later, take the jar. Make sure you are relaxed and ready. Empty your mind of all thoughts by counting down from twenty to one slowly with your out-breaths. When you reach one, open the lid and whatever thought, image, or idea enters your mind will be the key to your success.

Now say, **"Ahurani, I invite you to help me fulfill my goals, to bring me inspiration and realistic ambitions for my dreams. When I take off the lid of this magic jar, all will be revealed. "**

NEW MOON SPELL

A SPELL FOR WEIGHT LOSS

There's no simple way to lose weight by using magic, but it can certainly harness the power of Aphrodite to help your own inner magic to work so that you can change your diet, come to terms with personal issues, feel motivated to exercise, and so on. Aphrodite was the goddess of love, but also beauty and vanity. Her body was her shrine, and by invoking her powers, your body too will be blessed with the perfect figure that's right for you.

lace the mirror where you can see your reflection as you sit before the table. First, place a little lavender oil on your fingers and gently rub the oil down the sides of the white candle. Next, light the candle, take a piece of white quartz crystal in each hand, and say the following,

> *"Aphrodite, Lady of*
> *confidence*
> *Love, esteem, and vanity,*
> *Please help me to see my*
> *inner beauty*
> *Reflected before me*
> *And to restore my integrity*
> *Of self-love, body, and soul."*

Place the quartz crystals in front of the mirror, one to represent your body, the other to represent your desire to lose weight. While the white candle burns, write down the things in your life that make you crave food.

Last, write down these empowering enchantments:

> *"Food has no power over me."*

> *"My self-respect and self-love are mine."*

> *"I deserve to shine my beauty on the world."*

Gaze at yourself in the mirror and say the charms nine times. Then thank Aphrodite for her help, relax for nine minutes while the candle burns down, and blow it out. Place the two pieces of quartz crystal under your pillow to empower you with the determination to succeed in your goal. Every night before you go to bed—until you reach your desired weight—repeat the three empowerment enchantments as you gaze at yourself in a mirror.

WHAT YOU WILL NEED

A hand mirror

Lavender oil

1 white candle

2 pieces of white quartz crystal

A piece of paper and a pen

FULL MOON SPELL

A SPELL TO GET WHAT YOU WANT

The full moon is always a time to reap rewards and finalize unfinished business. It's also a great time to focus on a goal when the moon is at its fullest, most flourishing light. This spell calls on the moon's vibrant, illuminating energy to send the tides of change working in your favor.

ight your incense on your altar or a table. Place the three pieces of red carnelian (symbolizing Mars, Fire, and Aries) in a triangle shape. Now take the piece of carnelian from the top point of the triangle in your hand, close your eyes, and imagine what you want. Once you have visualized your success story in your head, open your eyes and place the carnelian back on the table. Next, pick up the piece of carnelian at the

bottom right of the triangle and do the same thing, but this time as you see your desire, say,

> *"I believe in my intended deed, And with this crystal, Mars, and Fire, I will succeed."*

Finally, take up the last piece of carnelian and as you visualize your success, say,

> *"Begin my quest from this day forth and it will succeed. And with this crystal, Mars, and Fire, my dream fulfilled."*

From now on, every day for a month take the three pieces of carnelian with you wherever you go, either in a pouch or just in your pocket, to reinforce the energy you have invoked from this day and to help you to truly succeed and manifest the dream.

WHAT YOU WILL NEED

Frankincense incense

3 pieces of red carnelian

KEEP YOUR EYES OFF MY LOVER SPELL

To prevent your lover's eyes from wandering from your own lovely ones, you will simply cast a spell that will repel all other love interests. This spell invokes the power of the water nymph Melusine, who medieval legend tells was cursed and transformed into a serpent. Only if a knight kissed her would she return to her beautiful form. But every knight who saw her was repelled by her serpent form, so she cast a spell on each one as he left so that none would ever be loved by another woman.

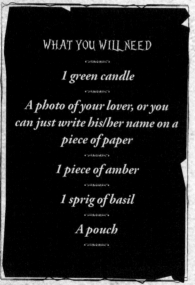

WHAT YOU WILL NEED

1 green candle

A photo of your lover, or you can just write his/her name on a piece of paper

1 piece of amber

1 sprig of basil

A pouch

or all the spells in this book to work, belief is essential. So believe, believe, and thrice believe what you are saying during the spell, and with that kind of intention, things that you want to happen will happen.

Light the green candle, and while holding the image or name of your lover, chant these words:

" I call upon the powers of
Melusine's attraction
To now work in reverse,
To repel all others
From my lover's eyes
No longer to be cursed."

Blow out the candle and then place the amber and the basil in the pouch at a window for one night, beside the name or photo of your lover. Soon your lover will only have eyes for you.

MONEY SPELL

This enchantment for attracting money calls on the popular Hindu god of wise abundance, Ganesha. His magic powers will remove all obstacles in your pathway to making money, which will help to manifest your dreams.

On your table or altar, place the small mirror in the bottom of the bowl and add about 1 cup (235 ml) of water. Then place the candles in the water and light them. Next, surround your bowl with the red flowers. Take time to relax and then gaze into the mirror in the bowl.

Next, hold your hands with palms down over the bowl of candles (far enough away not to be burned or get hot!) and feel the energy from the reflected light. As you do this, repeat this spell three times:

"Oh, Ganesha, what was once lacking, it is time, What was once wanting, will be mine, What was once one, will become tenfold, What was once tenfold, will be hundredfold, What was once hundredfold, will become Wealth and love to all around."

Relax, take a few slow deep breaths, and blow out the candles. Within a few weeks you will begin to reap the rewards of your efforts.

WHAT YOU WILL NEED

A small hand mirror

A clear glass bowl

Spring water

3 white floating candles

Red flowers such as camellias (Ganesha's symbol), carnations, or roses

Chapter 5
APRIL
Spells and Enchantments for New Beginnings

Theme:
Beginnings

Plant Energy:
Daisy for a Fresh Start and New Projects

Crystal Power:
Diamond for Clarity and Empowering Goals

ACCORDING TO THE ENGLISH POET T. S. ELIOT, APRIL IS A TURNING
POINT, AT WHICH THE PAST AND THE FUTURE ARE SEEN AS ONE;
WHEN, IN NORTHERN CLIMES AT LEAST, LILAC BUSHES BURST INTO
BLOOM ON DUSTY WASTE GROUND OR BESIDE RAILWAY TRACKS AS
THE RAIN BRINGS TO LIFE NEW GROWTH.

The month was named Aprilis by the Romans, but the origins of the name are still obscure. The traditional belief of its origin stems from the Latin verb *aperire*, "to open," an allusion to trees and flowers beginning to open, or to flower from buds. Since some of the Roman months were named in honor of divinities, and as April was sacred to the goddess Venus, it has also been suggested that Aprilis was originally Venus's month, from an ancient combination of her Greek goddess name, Aphrodite, to arrive at her springtime aspect as Aphrilis.

As the sun continues to make its way through the zodiac, it stays in Aries until about the 20th. The first part of the month is still about a feisty, "let's get things done" energy. This period is about action and is filled with self-motivated people who are as self-centered and conceited as the fiery influence of Mars. But as the sun moves across the cusp of Taurus, the energy changes to that of Venus. Venus rules Taurus, complementing this earth sign's symbols of beauty, vanity, good looks, attraction, seduction, feminine wiles, and the concerns of the body and sexuality.

In the late Middle Ages throughout the fashionable European courts, favored sorcerers and witches concocted aphrodisiacs, potions, and poisons, particularly in April, thought to be a month auspicious for providing male heirs. The tradition of celebrating virility, along with the magical generation of sexual stamina and subsequent fertility, were themes based on the ancient fertility festivities in pagan Europe as the first of May approached. The first few weeks of April were ruled by the virile ram god, followed by the fertile cow goddess, both symbols of various pagan cultures and still invoked by modern-day witches. This is why April is a month where desires quicken, the heat rises, and the tonic is needed to leave memories behind and start afresh. The spells for April are therefore all about moving on and beginning a new way of living, loving, or just being.

THE MEGALISIA

A SPELL FOR A FRESH NEW YOU

Magna Mater, the Roman goddess of world order, was usually depicted with tame lions beside her, and her feast was celebrated to acknowledge the power of the gods over mortals. The Megalisia marked the start of the new season of the agricultural year, and Magna Mater's benefits included protection from negative influences and flourishing new growth. You can tap into Magna Mater's energy to inspire you and bring you spirited energy.

 ight the candle and invite the goddess Magna Mater to join you. "Welcome, Magna Mater. Please join me as I remove all negativity from my life to be empowered with divine and cosmic spirit."

On one piece of paper, draw a pentagram (see page 15).

Write on the other piece of paper a list of things that you want to banish from your life: for example, fear, addictive behavior, irrational thoughts, frustration, worry, low self-esteem, self-sabotaging behavior, jealousy, possessiveness, poverty, hopelessness, lethargy, depression, and so on. Now hold the paper in your hands and say,

WHAT YOU WILL NEED

A white candle

2 pieces of paper

A black pen

A cauldron or metal cooking pot

1 piece of white quartz crystal

*"From the lion's paws,
comes Magna's charm.
Here on my path she'll be
my sweet balm
For her wisdom is great, her
protection secure
With her banishing power
I will become pure."*

In the candle flame, light the paper with the negative words and drop it into the cauldron. As it burns, relax and close your eyes. Imagine and feel your negativity burning away with it. Once most of the paper has burned away, blow out the candle.

Now say,

*"Thanks be to Magna
Mater's light
All is now banished into
the night."*

Place the white quartz crystal (invokes the power of the universe) in the center of the pentagram and say,

*"Thank you, Magna
Mater, for leading me away
from the dark into
the light."*

Leave the stone on the pentagram for four weeks (a lunar cycle) to ensure Magna Mater's magic works for you.

Over the next few days, find that all the negative thoughts you once had turn to positive ones, and you can start any new enterprise free of worries from the past.

SONGKRAN FESTIVAL

ENCHANTMENT TO BENEFIT ANY NEW PROJECTS

Songkran, meaning "astrological passage," is celebrated in Thailand for the traditional New Year, which falls around the 13th to 15th of April. The festival originally honored Phra-In, the god of wealth and king of the gods. It is said that once Brahma lost his head in a wager with Phra-In (Indra in Hindu mythology), the head was handed to the safekeeping of seven goddesses. As they passed the head from one to another, it signaled the start of the new year. Phra-In's appearance at the Songkran festival indicates future weather trends. If he is armed, the year ahead will be stormy; if he carries a torch, it signifies hot weather; a pot foretells rain; and a wand indicates calm days and little rain.

During the festival, Thai people throw water down the streets and toss water at each other; in fact, cities and villages are filled with water festival parties, famous throughout Southeast Asia. You too are going to celebrate Phra-In's rain-bringing powers, but in a purely magical way. With Phra-In's magic, you can achieve a fresh start in business or lifestyle, where the symbolic rains bring you financial benefits, prosperous living, good luck, and blessings.

WHAT YOU WILL NEED

A bowl of spring water

A bowl of rice

A bowl of your favorite fruit

1 piece of green tourmaline

To honor Phra-In, first sprinkle some of the spring water all around the floors of your home. It should be just enough to seem like gentle rain, the kind you would imagine being right for a good harvest. If you have outside space, do the same outside too; this invokes the rain god.

At the entrance to your home, place the bowl of rice (a symbol of happiness), the bowl of fruit (symbolizes the element Earth), and the piece of green tourmaline (enhances vitality and courage). Leave them all day as an offering of welcome to the prosperity and wealth of Phra-In. In the evening, remove your offerings and place the green tourmaline under your pillow for the night.

The god's magic will begin to work into your life over the next few days; the longer you leave the green tourmaline beneath your pillow, the more powerful the magic and the better the results.

April 14
GANGAUR FESTIVAL

SPELL FOR NEW ROMANCE, MARRIAGE, AND MOVING ON

In Rajasthan, India, the Gangaur is one of the most important festivals. It is celebrated by women who worship the goddess Gauri, who was a reincarnation of Parvati, the consort of the god Shiva. To invoke Gauri's magic for new beginnings and marital fidelity, women draw figures of the sun, moon, flowers, and other geometrical designs on their hands and feet.

 angaur is also worshipped by unmarried girls with a desire to get a handsome, loving, or noble partner, and they believe that if they are well-dressed while praying, they will be granted a good husband. So likewise, this spell is about dressing up in all your finery to invoke Gauri's blessing for future relationships. (However, this spell doesn't ensure a perfect marriage.)

WHAT YOU WILL NEED

Your finest clothes

5 gold-colored bracelets

5 white candles

An earthenware pot

5 white flowers

Washable face paint or pens you can use on your skin

First, dress in your finest clothes and wear your precious jewelry. As you do so, stare in the mirror and tell yourself that you are going to have the most spectacular marriage, new romance, or new beginning ever.

Place the five golden bracelets in a circle on the table or your altar and place the five white candles in the center of each bangle; these are all items associated with Parvati. Now place the earthenware pot in the middle of the circle and the white flowers inside. (These represent the treasures of Gauri.)

Light the candles, and as they burn and flicker, draw on the top of your left foot the symbol of the sun (a circle with a dot in the middle) and on your right foot the symbol of the moon (a crescent moon).

Next, repeat the following invocation to draw on Gauri's powers.

"Oh, Gauri, let this happiness be mine.
It can't be changed by wiles or rue.
With your help and magic true
By sun and moon, and all the stars
This spell brings fresh starts all anew."

Repeat this five times (Gauri's magic number), and for each chant, draw another sun and moon on your feet, until you have a total of five suns and five moons.

When you have performed the ritual, blow out the candles and keep the symbols on your feet for at least twenty-four hours for the magic to work.

April 28

THE FLORALIA

SPELL FOR CREATIVE LOVE

In ancient Rome, the Floralia was a pleasure-seeking festival held in honor of Flora, the ancient goddess of flowers, vegetation, and fertility. The theme of the festival was simply enjoyment, sexuality, beauty, and the love of spring. Roman prostitutes danced naked and performed in mock gladiator combats, wine flowed, and garlands of flowers were thrown to the crowds by street entertainers, jugglers, and musicians. People wore brightly colored robes and decorated everything with flowers or doused themselves in erotic perfumes.

 o enhance your own beauty, fertility, and sexuality and attract someone to you for creative love, make yourself the following talisman and invoke the power of Flora into your life. Let her passion unite you with the one you love or an intended new romance.

Sit in a quiet place in a garden, park, or the countryside. Place the book and the flowers in front of you and dab the perfume on the inner side of both wrists, behind your ears, and the outer sides of your ankles (to generate a flow of the perfume energy around you before you begin).

Now take one flower from your bunch and gently pluck from it three petals. Place these inside the middle of the book—these will be pressed flowers after three or four weeks.

Take another three petals, one at a time, and blow each of them from your fingers. As the first petal lands on the ground, say,

"One for love."

With the next petal say,

"Two for desire."

With the next petal say,

"Three for passion and fire."

Don't pick them up; just leave them where they are, and the spell is cast, even if a breeze or sudden gust of wind moves them on. This is the magical natural energy of the day.

Now stand up and say,

" Blessings, Flora, this spell is cast Now my love must surely last. "

Take your book home and place it under a pile of heavy books or magazines. In a month's time, take out the three petals and place them in a locket or small pillbox as a charm for eternal romance with the one you love.

WHAT YOU WILL NEED

A very heavy, hardback book

A bunch of your favorite flowers, or whatever is in season

Rose or orange flower/neroli eau de toilette or essential oil

EVE OF BELTANE

AN ENCHANTMENT FOR STARTING NEW ENTERPRISES

In pagan Europe, Beltane marked the beginning of the pastoral summer season, when livestock were driven out to the summer pasture. Rituals were held to protect animals from harm, both natural and supernatural, and to encourage fertility and growth.

 ature spirits were thought to be especially active at Beltane. The symbol of fire was used to benefit growth and to call on the spirits of nature and the waxing power of the sun to bring a creative beginning to the season.

On the eve of Beltane, this spell harnesses the spirits of nature and the energy of the sun to benefit you in any new enterprise or creative endeavor for the months ahead. It will also prepare you for tomorrow's May Day and Beltane celebrations, an important point in a Wiccan or witch's calendar.

WHAT YOU WILL NEED

A large piece of paper and a pen

A cauldron or cooking pot

5 twigs, preferably from 5 different species of trees: oak, rowan, elder, hazel, and willow. (If you can't find them, take photos or images of them from a book or the Internet and paste them onto separate pieces of paper.)

Spirit

Air

Water

Fire

Earth

On your main piece of paper, draw a pentacle: a five-pointed star within a circle, with the fifth point to the north or top of the circle.

Write the magic elemental words between each of the points as follows:

To left of the top point, "Spirit."
To the right of the top point, "Air."
Above the bottom right point, "Fire."
Between the two bottom points, "Earth." Above the bottom left point, "Water."

Now place the five twigs into the cauldron or cooking pot and with an imaginary wand encircle the cauldron five times and say,

The spirits of the woods, trees, and waters will now be there to help you activate any new enterprise in the coming months.

"Five woods into the Cauldron go
Burn them fast and burn them slow.
When the wheel begins to turn
Soon the Beltane fires will burn.
Where the rippling waters go
Cast a stone, the truth you'll know.
These Eight words the Rede fulfill
'An Ye Harm None, Do What Ye Will.'"

NEW MOON SPELL

A SPELL TO KICK AN OLD HABIT AND START AFRESH

April is Venus's month, and invoking the power of Venus will help you to rid yourself of past habits. Venus talismans (pendants or rings inscribed with attributes of Venus) were worn by Romans not only to deflect the influence of envious or jealous rivals in love, but to banish all past bad influences too, rather like the use of talismans to ward off the "evil eye."

For this enchantment, you are symbolically a channel or conduit between time past and future; the present "you" needs to be protected, so first walk in a large clockwise circle with your hand outstretched and pointing at the earth to create a magic circle around you.

As you do so, say,

"I cast this magic circle and am safe between two worlds."

Now within your magic circle, place the five white candles (to represent the five magical elements) in a circle and light them. Then say,

"By the power of earth, fire, water, and air,
Out with the old, in with the new
Blessing, oh Venus, for all that I do
To let go of the past and all that is bad
And empower me with grace and all that is glad."

Sprinkle the water on each of the candles. Finally, blow out the candles, and all past habits you want to leave behind will disappear. In the next few weeks, you can move on from the chains of the past.

WHAT YOU WILL NEED

5 white candles

A small bowl of spring water

FULL MOON SPELL

ZEUS AND PANDIA SPELL FOR BENEFICIAL LUCK

In Greek mythology, Zeus was the god who decided whether you had good or bad luck in life. As long as you made offerings to him, he usually bestowed you with good luck. His affair with the moon goddess Selene resulted in their beautiful daughter, Pandia, who was worshipped for her beneficial powers on the night of the full moon (believed to be the moment of her birth). Invoke both Zeus's and Pandia's powers of luck and success on the eve of the full moon.

lace and light the red candle, a symbol of potency, on the table, with the two stones on either side of the candle; the lapis lazuli is for hidden power and the turquoise is for exploiting ideas. Sit quietly before the table or altar on the eve of the full moon. Begin to unravel the string from the ball until it is as long as your arm. Then cut the string, place the length on the table, and say,

"By Pandia's power of moonlit night
Come bring me all that is my right.
And as this twine is cut each time
The luck of Zeus will be mine."

Repeat the string cutting nine more times (Zeus's number), saying the above spell each time.

When you have finished, say,

"Thank you, Zeus and Pandia, for helping me to have all that is due to me and for luck and stability in the future."

Leave the threads on the table overnight, but don't forget to blow out the candle! In the morning, take the threads and wrap them in a silk scarf. Keep them in a safe place so that you are blessed with good luck and long-term happiness.

WHAT YOU WILL NEED

1 red candle

1 piece of lapis lazuli

1 piece of turquoise

A ball of string

A pair of scissors

A silk scarf

SPELL TO BANISH UNWANTED ATTENTION

Rather like using a charm to ward off the evil eye, this simple little enchantment will stop your unwanted admirer in his or her tracks. However, you must truly be gentle when doing this spell, because if you have any resentment or malice in your heart . . . remember that in the witch's law book, what goes around comes around.

 n the piece of paper, write a list of the positive attributes of the person you want to deter, such as his or her job, home, or leisure pursuits—write whatever comes to mind, so long as what you write is not negative.

Next, light your black candle and sit quietly before the flame as you repeat this enchantment seven times:

*"The Stars above, the Stone below
Extinguish these flames of love right now.
With Earth it rises o'er our heads
With Air it empties both our beds.
With Water, gold and Vitriol
We will be parted forever so.
Great Heavens, Stars, and Oceans pure
Take away unwanted desire
To never come to me again
And then this spiral flame will end."*

Finally wrap the paper around the black obsidian stone and bury it in the garden or somewhere outside where no one can find it. As you bury it, say,

"Thus ends this infatuation so mote it be."

You will be free from the attention of the one you do not want in your life by the next full moon.

WHAT YOU WILL NEED

A piece of paper and a pen

1 black candle

1 piece of black obsidian

SPELL TO ENSURE YOU ACHIEVE YOUR GOAL

This spell first stops rivals from blocking or preventing you from your goal and means that any form of achievement can be all yours. This spell calls on the spirits of nature and spring to sprinkle you with their blessings to achieve your best.

On the piece of paper, write down the names of those people you want to block, then cross out their names and write your own in much larger writing across all their names. As you do so, say,

"I cross you, I banish you
I cover you, I command you
All who do not deserve to
have luck with me
Be gone now, so mote it be."

Take the purple candle and rub a little lavender oil down the sides of the candle to bless it. Place the paper of names on a dish and the candle on top of the paper, then light the candle.

While the candle is burning, take the basil sprigs in your hands and pick as many leaves as there are names on your banishment list. Basil is protective, restorative, generative, and empowering, and it keeps away unwanted spirits, people, and energies.

As you do so, say,

"As nature stirs again
I ask the spirits of spring
to bless me with personal
achievement and success
See that it comes to me,
and me alone."

Blow out the candle, place the basil leaves in a paper bag, and throw the bag into the trash. This symbolic action means you will now achieve all you set out to do alone, without the interference of anyone you have written on your list.

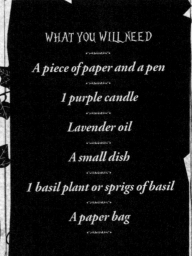

WHAT YOU WILL NEED

A piece of paper and a pen

1 purple candle

Lavender oil

A small dish

1 basil plant or sprigs of basil

A paper bag

Chapter 6
MAY

Spells and Enchantments for Body, Beauty, and Sex

Theme:
Body Beautiful

Plant Energy:
Hawthorn for Fertility

Crystal Power:
Emerald for Sexual Charisma

IN THE NORTHERN HEMISPHERE, THE OLD RHYME GOES, "MAY BRINGS FLOCKS OF PRETTY LAMBS, SKIPPING BY THEIR FLEECY DAMS", AND INDEED THERE IS NOW A FEELING OF BLOSSOMING AND GROWTH. IN EUROPE, THE HAWTHORN BURSTS INTO FLOWER AND FIELDS ARE GREEN AGAIN. IN THE SOUTHERN HEMISPHERE, AUTUMN HAS WELL AND TRULY ARRIVED, AND WITH WINTER APPROACHING, SOME PEOPLE HEAD FOR NORTHERN CLIMES TO SEEK OUT THE WARMER SUN.

 he month of May appears to have been named in honor of the Greek goddess Maia, who was identified with the Romans' goddess of fertility, Bona Dea. Maia was the daughter of Atlas and was the eldest of the seven Pleiades born on Mount Cyllene in Arcadia, and she was also the mother of the Greek god Hermes.

As the sun moves on through the zodiac, May's first three weeks are dedicated to Taurus, the sign of the bull. Taurean magic is "sympathetic magic"; in other words, it uses correspondences in nature in tandem with the deities who respond to that natural world. Taurus is ruled by the planet and goddess Venus. All Venusian pursuits—such as love, pleasure, sensuality, and pampering one's body—are now favored. The magical energy is right for boosting your sexual power and attraction, working with the senses, and getting in tune with your feminine side.

As the sun moves into Gemini around the 21st, the energy now changes to a lighter, romantic vibration. Communication usually improves, and people are more willing to open up, relax, and get on with life. This is a lighthearted energy, where the future is more exciting and inspiring than dwelling on the past. The energy is right for making amends, learning a new subject, being a jack-of-all-trades, and for trading ideas with and transmitting knowledge to others.

Gemini is also a fast-moving energy. It can be equated to a flock of birds, as ideas swoop in and out of the creative witch's book of shadows. Those born under the sign are usually quick to read between the lines, quick to see the truth behind illusion, and are often good tricksters themselves! During the Gemini cycle, magic spells can still be cast for body, sex, and beauty, but they are now for fun, fitness, or the romantic, seductive, crazy side of life. May is the month for employing magic spells that will enhance all of the senses, including your common sense. With your mind, body, and soul in good shape, you will be fit for the summer ahead.

May 1
BELTANE

A SPELL FOR PERFECT SEXUAL HARMONY

The well-known May Day celebration of dancing around the maypole is part of a much more mysterious and ancient Celtic fertility celebration known as Beltane. Traditionally, Beltane began when the hawthorn tree, also known as the May tree, blossomed. It is the tree of sexuality and fertility and the classic flower with which to decorate a maypole. It was both worn and used to decorate the home at Beltane.

This spell draws on the powers of the May god and goddess. It will increase your seductive powers tenfold and put you in touch with your true sexual needs.

Draw a symbol of the sun (circle with a dot in the center) at the top of the paper and a symbol of the moon (crescent moon) at the bottom of the paper, to represent the union of the Green Man and the May goddess, Flora. In the middle of the paper draw a large circle and within the circle write the following spell:

"By the power of the God and Goddess twice
We are united, in love, in physical embrace
And in our sexuality."

WHAT YOU WILL NEED

A piece of paper

A pen or pencil

A box with a lid

7 pieces of red garnet

7 white candles

Sprigs of hawthorn blossom, or if unavailable, an image of hawthorn blossom

Fold the paper four times and place it in your special box. This will disperse all negative energy, envy, jealousy, or spite from anyone around you, so that you are ready for perfect sexual harmony with the one you love. Close the lid and place in a south-facing window to maximize the power of Flora and the Green Man.

Next, in the southeast corner of your bedroom, place one piece of garnet to inspire romance and passionate love. Place another garnet under your pillow to ignite intimacy and place the remaining five pieces on your table or altar in a circle.

Light the seven white candles, placing three to the right of the circle, three to the left, and the seventh in the middle. Gaze into the flame of the middle candle, concentrate on your lover or intended one, and repeat this spell.

"By the power of the Sacred Marriage
I anoint true love with this sacred wine
For sexual potency and desire
Will be all yours, and mine."

Now place the sprigs or image of hawthorn blossom on top of your box. For the magic to work, leave the garnets in place for as long as you desire. Remove the hawthorn blossom or its image before the next evening and bury it under a tree or bush (or even in a flowerpot) for the magic of the goddess and Green Man to improve your sex life.

May 5
AMATERASU'S FESTIVAL

SPELL TO BE BEAUTIFUL

Amaterasu was the ancient Shinto sun goddess, who bestowed the blessing of beauty and grace on those who worshipped her daily journey across the skies. Her name means "illuminating heaven." One of her legends tells of how, because of the treachery of her brother, the moon, she hid in a cave for so long that there was no longer any light on earth. She was persuaded to come out only when tricked by the other gods, who left a mirror hanging from a tree. When she peeped out to see what was going on, she saw a reflection of herself in the mirror, and, thinking this was a goddess more beautiful than herself, she stormed out of the cave to confront the rival. In doing so, she brought light to the world again. It is this sacred mirror that is said to be kept at the Ise Shrine in Honshu, Japan.

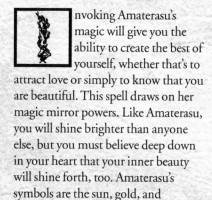

Invoking Amaterasu's magic will give you the ability to create the best of yourself, whether that's to attract love or simply to know that you are beautiful. This spell draws on her magic mirror powers. Like Amaterasu, you will shine brighter than anyone else, but you must believe deep down in your heart that your inner beauty will shine forth, too. Amaterasu's symbols are the sun, gold, and the mirror.

WHAT YOU WILL NEED

A hand mirror

Go out for a walk and take the hand mirror with you. Find a café or bench and sit for a while. If the sun isn't shining, imagine it beaming down on you, the solar energy and Amaterasu's magic filling you with light. Take the mirror from your bag and gaze at yourself, even if there are people around you.

Say to yourself, out loud or in your head,

"I am the sun, I am the goddess of the sun, and I am beautiful."

Realize that you are someone special, and then place the mirror back in your bag and walk home.

When you are back in your home, take the mirror and reflect light into every corner of every room. This is the energy you have gathered from the sun, which will empower every inch of your space with magical beauty. You will now be blessed with Amaterasu's qualities and will shine as brightly as she does.

SUN MOVES INTO GEMINI

ENCHANTMENT FOR YOUTHFULNESS

The sun's move into Gemini changes the energy, and the world is lightened from sensual passion to a time of fun and frolics. The Gemini twins symbolize youthfulness, and it is the perfect time to attend to your fitness, not only to look good, but to think and feel good and know you are in shape. This spell won't change you overnight, but it will give you the power to make your body, mind, spirit, and soul as young at heart as you want yourself to be.

 In ancient Greece, ribbons or long pieces of cloth were braided or knotted to invoke one's own personal energy as part of the spell, rather than just calling on the gods. At each knot or crossing, a flower was entwined to mark part of the spell; one flower for body, one for mind, one for soul, one for love, one for youthfulness, and so on. This spell works on this principle, so that each knot you make is a symbol of your youthful new self.

Braid the three strands of ribbon together with five crossings and knot the end. If you don't know how to make a three-strand braid, then just make five knots along the lengths of ribbon.

WHAT YOU WILL NEED

3 lengths (about 3 feet [90 cm] long) of yellow ribbon (Gemini's color)

1 piece of lavender or a lavender pillow

Between your hands, take hold of the
first crossing or knot and say, *"Gemini's magic is a potent way*
For the youthfulness I wish today."

Move your hands on to the next
crossing or knot and say, *"Oh, Gemini, ribbons help my body be fit*
Braided this way, let the spell be writ."

Move your hands to the third crossing
or knot and say, *"Let the spell grow and my health improve*
Thrice times this number my body be true."

On the fourth crossing say,

"By the grace of the planets this spell be worked
And my fitness and youthfulness ever alert."

On the final knot or crossing say,

"Bound again the spell begins
When in two weeks untied, the spell will be mine."

Keep the braided or knotted ribbons
in a drawer with your clothes
and place a piece of lavender or a
lavender pillow in the same place to
enhance the magical qualities of your
enchantment. Two weeks later, untie
the braid or knots and you will be
blessed with a youthful aura and can
arrive at the level of fitness that you
hope to achieve.

May 29
OAK APPLE DAY

A SPELL TO RESTORE HOLISTIC HEALTH

In May 1660, with the restoration of the English monarchy and Charles II's accession to the throne, a new celebration, Oak Apple Day, was granted to commemorate the king's escape from the Roundhead army when he hid in an oak tree after the Battle of Worcester in 1651. Anyone who failed to wear a sprig of oak risked being pelted with birds' eggs or thrashed with nettles!

Those who used magic spells, healing herbs, and other traditional remedies knew the value of the oak tree and its powerful symbol of longevity, strength, and stability. There was an ancient Welsh belief that good health was maintained by rubbing your hands on a piece of oak, and that dew found under oak trees was a magical beauty aid. In seventeenth-century England, witches preferred to call themselves "cunning folk"; one Londoner, known as Arthur Gauntlet, wrote a grimoire called *A Cunning Man's Book of Charms*. This spell is based on one of his cunning charms.

WHAT YOU WILL NEED

A handful of lavender flowers

Lavender oil

An image of an oak tree

One acorn

Fill your bathtub with warm water and put the lavender flowers and a few drops of the lavender oil into the water. (Doing so maximizes your ability to be at one with the elements of nature.) Place the image of the oak tree where you will be able to see it from your bathtub.

Hold the acorn in your right hand and say these words:

*"Cleanse my spirit,
cleanse my soul
Enrich my life and make
me whole."*

Place the acorn beside the picture of the oak tree, then climb into the bath and relax, breathing in the scent of the lavender. Gaze at the imagery of your oak tree and keep repeating to yourself how strong, secure, and beautiful the tree is. Then think of your life in that way too: safe, secure, and whole.

Leave the oak tree image and the acorn overnight. The following morning, place them on your altar or table and then take the acorn between your hands and as you do, say,

*"This oak tree strong,
this oak tree proud
Will always hold us
in the ground.
Blessed oak, sacred oak
So mote it be."*

Keep the acorn in a special box, and you will feel whole and strong as an oak tree. If you ever feel weak or unwell, hold the acorn again and repeat the last part of the spell to restore your strength.

FLORES DE MAYO

ENCHANTMENT FOR CHARISMA

The Flores de Mayo is a Catholic flower festival held in the Philippines that incorporates traditional Filipino religious traditions. Sisina was the ancient Filipino goddess of beauty and love; she was garlanded with flowers that blossom in May and was worshipped to increase fertility and self-love. At the feast, a place is often laid for her at the table, and her symbols include the whitest doves' eggs that can be found.

 This magic charm works to bring Sisina's magic to life in your home and to give you the seductive powers and charisma you deserve.

First, you need to prepare the egg by blowing out the inside. Using the thick needle, carefully pierce a hole in both ends of the egg, making one hole larger than the other. Push the needle into the egg yolk gently and swirl it around carefully to break up the yolk. Hold the end of the

WHAT YOU WILL NEED

1 large, white egg

A thick needle

A drinking straw

Red paint or a red pen

White embroidery thread or thin wool thread

drinking straw to the smaller hole and blow through the larger hole to push out the egg white and yolk. Try doing this with the bottom hole facing the floor to let gravity help you! Leave the egg to dry out overnight.

When your egg is empty and thoroughly dried out, paint or draw five pentagrams (see page 15) on the egg.

When the paint has dried, prepare it for hanging by threading the thin thread (white to honor Sisina) through the two holes and secure it with a large knot at one end.

Clear your mind of other thoughts, relax, focus on your desire for charisma, and say,

Now hang or attach the egg in front of a mirror, where it will reflect and magnify your charisma back to you. This way you can invoke Sisina's magical powers every day you look at yourself in the mirror.

"Little charm made of shell
As you rest here all be well.
May charisma flow to me
May Sisina's power encompass me
May all I do and think and be
Be blessed with grace and love
So mote it be."

NEW MOON SPELL FOR BETTER SEX

This charm uses the power of the lucky horseshoe, which is associated with virility. It was used among French country folk during the fifteenth century as a talisman to restore the sex drives of weary soldiers returning home from the wars.

Place the horseshoe—with the curve at the bottom—on your altar or table. Bless the shoe with the oils by simply wiping a little of each fragrance onto the horseshoe.

As you do so, say,

> "By the anointing of
> this shoe
> Soon my love will be
> perfumed
> With virile spice and
> passion high.
> No one can stop our
> love's desire."

Next, wind the red and blue threads (representing male and female power, respectively) around the horseshoe. Make three knots to hold them in place, and each time you make a knot, whisper to yourself what your greatest sexual secret desire is.

Hold the shoe in your hands, close to your heart, and say,

> "By the holding of
> this shoe
> The power of desire takes
> over too.
> We will not stop from
> dusk till dawn
> With lovers' heat and
> sex reborn."

Use the nails or screws to hang the horseshoe above your bedroom door with the opening of the shoe to the top. From now on, your love life will be blessed with pure passion and fulfilling sex.

WHAT YOU WILL NEED

A horseshoe

Tuberose perfume or essential oil

Gardenia perfume or essential oil

Jasmine perfume or essential oil

Red and blue silk threads

2 nails or 2 screws

FULL MOON SPELL FOR BANISHING FEARS

Just after the full moon, this spell will help you overcome any fears you have, swapping fear for opportunities to be seized.

he sacred book can be any book you value—a Bible, a much-loved sacred text, or a novel that has "changed" you in some way.

Place the book on your table or altar and randomly open it to a page. Don't look at the page yet. Light the incense to banish all forms of stress, worry, and difficult emotions.

Now ring the bell three times to cast out unwanted fears. Place it back on the table and sit before your book. Close your eyes and with one finger, begin to make circles in the air over the open book. When you feel compelled to stop, place your finger randomly on the page. Open your eyes and look to where your finger is pointing. Take the whole sentence, or even two sentences together, and write them down on a piece of paper.

These words are an oracle and will banish all fear from you forever if you keep the paper in a safe place. If ever you feel fearful, read the words again or perform the spell again.

WHAT YOU WILL NEED

A sacred book

Frankincense incense

An iron or metal bell

A piece of paper and a pen

HEALTHY LIFE SPELL

We all want to be healthier. This spell won't cure you from any disease or ailment, nor will it stop you from catching a common cold, but its magical properties will boost your holistic health.

lace the three basil leaves and angelica powder in the bowl. Prick your finger with the needle and let a drop of blood fall onto the powder.

Do not mix the magic potion or touch it, but simply say the following:

"As without, so within
As above, so below
As with soul,
so with skin
As with spirit,
so with blood."

Now light the white candle and drip a few drops of wax onto your mixture by tipping the candle at an angle.

Now say,

"As with energy,
so with flow
As with blood,
so with sweat
As with body,
so with spirit
So with my soul's wealth
now enriched
So my body's health
will flourish."

At some point in the next three days, empty the contents of your magic potion into a stream, river, or the sea.

Within one lunar cycle, you should feel the energy you need for a healthier lifestyle. If not, repeat the spell, but most of all believe, believe, and believe it as you perform the charm.

WHAT YOU WILL NEED

3 basil leaves

1 teaspoon angelica root powder

A small glass dish or bowl

A sterilized needle

1 white candle

JUNE, NAMED AFTER THE ROMAN GODDESS JUNO, HAS ALWAYS BEEN A TRADITIONAL MONTH FOR MARRIAGE, ENGAGEMENTS, AND SETTLING DOWN. AS PROTECTOR OF WOMEN AND CHILDREN, JUNO RESTORES RELATIONSHIPS, HONORS MARRIAGE AND FIDELITY, AND HELPS WOMEN TO BE HAPPY IN WHATEVER ROLE THEY CHOOSE TO TAKE: MOTHER, WIFE, LOVER, OR UNATTACHED. SHE ALSO RULES WOMEN'S CYCLES AND IS OFTEN KNOWN AS THE "QUEEN OF HEAVEN."

 herever Juno went, she was attended by her messenger Iris (the Rainbow), who raced so quickly through the air that she was seldom seen, but left the radiant trail of her highly colored robes in the sky. In traditional folklore, the month of June has been associated with the dramatic rainbows seen across northern skylines.

June is considered a perfect month for marriage and is the month with the longest daylight hours of the year in the northern hemisphere and the shortest daylight hours of the year in the southern hemisphere. With the turning point of the solstice, June heralds the culmination of fertile energy in the north and the coming spring in the southern hemisphere.

The first part of June is capricious, friendly, and fun-loving. Working magic spells is aimed at enhancing one's goals and relationships and getting in balance all the things that were hoped for earlier in the year. With the solstice, celebrations fill the air, as traditional pagans, Wiccans, and other New Age mystics honor the solstice at sacred places throughout the world.

With the sun's move into Cancer, there is now a different quality. The magic is watery, sensual, and blessed by the power of the moon and the goddess Selene. The end of June is for roses, thunderstorms, shady arbors, and secret bowers where lovers embrace. The feeling is seductive, feminine, and enhanced by magical spells devoted to seduction and creating beneficial changes for your future.

With the powerful lunar influence, magic rituals with water, silver, or carrying or wearing moonstone will enhance all relationships. Spells cast under this lunar influence are self-empowering and long-lasting and can ensure that the rest of the summer will be how you want it to be. Like the Greek moon goddess, Selene, you too can seduce and lure anyone you choose. If white flowers are offered to Selene on the night of the new moon—i.e., when you see the first sliver of its crescent phase in the sky—a fortunate month will follow.

June 1–15

CHINESE DRAGON BOAT FESTIVAL

A SPELL TO BANISH NEGATIVITY
THIS SPELL CAN BE PERFORMED AT ANY POINT BETWEEN THE 1ST AND 15TH OF JUNE.

At some point during the first two weeks of June, depending on the lunar calendar, the Chinese hold a Dragon Boat Festival. This is a traditional holiday that commemorates the life and death of the third-century BCE Chinese scholar Qu Yuan. Falsely accused of conspiracy, he was exiled by the king and in his sorrow jumped into the Miluo River and drowned himself. The people of Chu tried to save him, but to no avail. Since then, the Dragon Boat Festival is celebrated to commemorate the villagers' attempt to rescue Qu Yuan.

raditionally, the festival included charms and talismans to banish evil in one's life and encourage positive energy. Part of the ritual was eating rice dumplings, drinking wine, and racing the homemade boats dressed or painted as beneficial dragons. Perfumed sachets were carried to ward off evil, and fetching "noon water," or water collected at noon, was a way to purify and cleanse the home. Today, people still wear talismans or hang pictures of the deity Zhong Kui on the door of their homes. Regarded as a vanquisher of ghosts and evil spirits, Zhong Kui had the power to command more than 80,000 demons. His image is often painted on household gates as a guardian spirit, and in business where high-value goods are involved.

This spell is a general spell to banish all negativity from your life by drawing on the power of Zhong Kui.

Place the black candle and other tools on a table or on the ground so everything is ready.

Before invoking the power of Zhong Kui, cast a circle around yourself and the magic tools and call in the spirits of the four quarters for protection as described on page 78.

Within your magic circle, light the candle and the incense and invite Zhong Kui to join you by saying,

"Zhong Kui, guardian of all, protector from negativity, please join me as I seek to banish all negative energy from my life."

Take up your wand or athame and point it at the chalice or goblet of water. Close your eyes and imagine a pure white light coming down from the sky, as you draw on the spirit powers. Repeat the following:

"By all Zhou's power and wondrous light Be gone all evil from my life All negative thoughts are sent away That positive ones will only stay."

Now sit down and write on the paper with your pen all the things you want to banish from your life. They may be emotions such as anger and jealousy or people whom you no longer want to know. They may be feelings of loss or problems with money or debt. Whatever it is that is negative about your life, write it down. Fold the paper up four times and place it beside the chalice. Now say,

"All negativity be gone All wrongs be gone All bad things be gone All that is dark be turned to light All that is night be turned to day All that is bright come to my life."

Next, pick up the chalice and drink some of the water, but not all of it. Place the paper into the rest of the sacred water, where you will leave it until noon the next day.

Release Zhou from the spell by saying,

"Thank you, Zhou, hunter of negativity, vanquisher of all that is dark or bad, thank you for helping me to move on."

Release the spirits by bowing to each of the four directions and giving thanks, then blow out the candle.

The next day, go back to where you left the chalice of water. Fetching spring water at noon was a Chinese magical charm to banish all negativity. Exactly at noon, take the paper out of the water, tear it up into shreds, and throw it away, then throw away the water. As you throw it away, you are ridding your life of everything bad.

WHAT YOU WILL NEED

1 black candle

Sandalwood incense

A wand, wooden stick, or athame

A chalice or goblet filled with water

A piece of paper

A black pen

MIDSUMMER'S DAY/ SOLSTICE

SPELL FOR HAPPY CHANGES

Like the winter solstice and the two equinoxes, the summer solstice is one of the most important days in the year for spell work. The day does vary each year according to the sun's path through the ecliptic, so please check on the Internet or in a diary which day the solstice falls for the year you do these spells. A turning point in the Wiccan calendar, the weeks and months leading up to "Litha," as it is known by neopagans, are when the sun gains maximum power and our attention turns to the material world, abundance in nature, and fertility. The name Litha is rooted in the Venerable Bede's description of two Anglo-Saxon names for the months of midsummer, early Litha and later Litha—months corresponding to June and July.

 idsummer is a time for purification and thanksgiving, as well as looking forward to the future. We can give thanks for the sunshine and fertility of the past few months and welcome the days where different magic harvests the rewards of the spells sown earlier in the year. This midsummer spell is made up of a ritual to honor the energy, which is best done in the morning of Midsummer's Day, and another spell to perform in the afternoon.

Lay out all the magical ingredients on the altar.

Sprinkle a little of the herbal oils or essences onto the flowers on your altar, then light the pink candles. Take a few moments to enjoy the fragrances and the flickering candle flames.

Pick up the athame or wand, hold it firmly in both hands, and visualize all the energy of the sun concentrated along its blade. It may be helpful to imagine a warm, golden light emanating from the blade.

Hold the athame blade directly above the bowl of fruit, pointing downward toward the fruit. Visualize the sun's energy passing from the blade into the fruit, which in turn becomes charged with golden energy.

Lay down the athame.

Eat the fruit slowly, giving thanks for the fertility of the sun, while visualizing the fulfillment of all your desires over the coming months. Finally, extinguish the candles.

In the afternoon, wear silver rings, diamonds, or white crystal jewelry and take a bath or shower using patchouli oil or white musk. All these attributes will imbue you with midsummer magic and augment your success for the next six months.

TURN TO PAGE 104 FOR THE AFTERNOON CHARM.

WHAT YOU WILL NEED

An altar or table decorated with summer flowers on a white cloth

Lemon balm, lavender, and elderflower essences/oils or perfume

5 pink candles

An athame or wand

A small bowl containing summer fruits you want to eat

Silver rings, diamonds, or white crystal jewelry

Patchouli oil or white musk

A metal goblet or bowl (preferably gold, silver, pewter, or copper colored)

A golden or silver-colored ring

5 white candles

Rose petals

3 cloves

AFTERNOON CHARM
SPELL FOR HAPPY CHANGES—CONTINUED FROM PAGE 103

After your ritual bath, take the metal goblet or bowl and the gold or silver ring. These represent Metal magic, the element needed to boost your charisma. Create a magic circle of five white candles and place the bowl/goblet and ring in the center. Next, sprinkle some rose petals into the bowl, followed by three cloves (a magical talisman to represent love, harmony, and peace).

Now light the candles, and as you watch the candles flicker for a few minutes, repeat the spell:

"I am a creature of nature's soul.
These talismans before me my only goal.
Let this midsummer joy my life unfold
And the days to come be as bright as gold."

Blow out the candles and look forward to the enriching months ahead.

GET BACK MY EX SPELL

MIDSUMMER'S DAY IS THE ONLY DAY IN THE YEAR
WHEN THIS SPELL WILL WORK.

You can pick out your locations beforehand, but you must place the roses, which represent true love, on Midsummer's Day. Bury one rose under the fruit tree, which represents the element Earth. Place another near the gate of the church, to represent the element Air; another near running water, to represent the element Water; and another one beside a crossroads, at the south corner, or whichever of the corners is nearest the south, to doubly enhance the power of Fire, the element which harnesses passion. The last rose goes under your own pillow.

Sleep with the rose under your pillow.

On the following day, pluck the petals from that rose and say,

"This power of love reach out and beyond
Of water, of earth, of air, and of fire.
Midsummer nymphs take my lover this light
To bring him back from this magical round
By his own will and desire, he will want to be mine."

Now, return to the four locations where you left the roses. Pluck three petals (to represent the union of two plus the power of love) from each rose at each location and scatter them at each location. Your ex will be back very soon, if you truly believe that your spell will work.

WHAT YOU WILL NEED

5 red roses

A fruit tree

A church

Natural moving water, like a stream, river, or the sea

A crossroads

SUN INTO CANCER

A SPELL FOR ENRICHMENT AND WEALTH

As the sun moves into the zodiac sign of Cancer around the 21st and 22nd, it marks a change of energy from the busy, fun-loving, up-tempo solar energy of Gemini, to lunar energy. Cancerian energy enhances our sense of belonging and gets us in touch with our feelings and how we can enrich our lives and achieve stability in all we do. As Cancer is ruled by the moon, it is also symbolic of security, wealth, and the spirit of enterprise. This charm draws on the power of the Celtic moon goddess, Arianrhod, whose name means "silver wheel" and who's identified with the wheel of the year and the web of fate.

 y invoking Arianrhod's powers, you will be ready to look to the future with fresh ideas to increase your wealth. If you believe you can make a fortune this year, you will, but you need to really believe it as you cast this spell.

Place the bowl, goblet, or chalice on a table, fill it nearly to the brim with natural spring water, and then sit quietly in front of it. Place your green crystal carefully at the bottom of the glass in the water. As you remove your hand from the water, with your index finger, draw a circle in a clockwise direction on the surface of the water as a magic circle of protection.

WHAT YOU WILL NEED

A glass bowl, goblet, or chalice

Natural spring water

1 piece of green tourmaline, jade, malachite, or aventurine

Close your eyes to calm your mind a little. When you are ready, open them and gaze into the water at the crystal, as if you are looking into your own future. Then say,

"Arianrhod, please join me in this rite of prosperity. Please bring me your gifts, and for the good of everyone around me too."

Now take the crystal out of the water and place it in a safe place in the southeast corner of your home. This is where beneficial solar energy aligns to the power of the crystal. You must leave the crystal here for nine days to charge your home with feminine lunar power, nine being associated with the nine months of pregnancy.

After nine days, remove the crystal, put it in a pouch, and carry it with you to bring you beneficial wealth in all ways.

June 28

THE SUMMANUS FEAST

SPELL TO MAKE YOUR FUTURE SIZZLE

In ancient Rome, Summanus was the god of nocturnal thunder, while Jupiter was the god of daytime thunder. Mount Summano was located in the Alps near Vicenza, Italy, and was believed to be the site of a thunder god cult dating back to the ninth century BCE. A deep grotto on the mountain was where a young shepherd girl got lost and disappeared forever. The god Summanus still appears at night, his mighty lightning bolts hitting the top of the mountain as he tries to light up the landscape and reveal the lost maiden's whereabouts. Offerings to Summanus included cakes made in the shape of his talisman, the wheel. He was propitiated at the end of June, when thunderstorms were particularly frequent, for a successful harvest.

WHAT YOU WILL NEED

1 white candle

2 silver-colored rings

A silver-colored box with a lid

A few drops of frankincense oil

2 white flowers

 By invoking the thunder god's magical energy, you too can lighten your future and see clearly how to make a sizzling success of all your greatest intentions.

Place the magical ingredients on your table or altar and light the white candle. Put the silver rings in the box and close it. Silver is precious to Summanus and is associated with lightning. Now say,

"I call on thee, oh Summanus,
To lighten my way to brilliant times
To show me where success will be
And all who share my goals to see
The best of harvests yet to come
With this special trust we shall be done."

Sprinkle the oil onto the two white flowers and place them on top of the box. With your finger, draw an imaginary cross over the box, then an imaginary circle around the cross, to symbolize the wheel of Summanus.

Leave the box and offerings for one week, then throw the flowers away. Wear the rings every day or place in a pouch and carry them with you until the success you are looking for manifests.

June 30

BELLONA'S FEAST

A SPELL TO GET YOUR WAY

The ancient Roman goddess of war, Bellona, was identified as the sister of Mars, or in some sources, she was his wife. Bellona's main attribute was a military helmet, and she usually held a sword, shield, or other battle weapon. In magic, you can invoke Bellona's power to fight against the odds, to get what you want, and to see the light at the end of the tunnel. Calling on Bellona to help you get what you want, in the nicest possible way, means you can achieve your aim without hurting anyone else in the process. Bellona's magic works through the placement of her magical crystals, which is the key to the success of this spell.

 irst, perform the following rituals with these pieces of crystal to reinforce the spell.

Onyx brings order and enhances the ability to be mistress of your own destiny where you are no longer tied to other people's schemes. Place a piece in the north-facing corner of your bedroom to maximize self-empowerment.

Carnelian placed just inside your front door will promote confidence and build self-esteem.

WHAT YOU WILL NEED

1 piece of onyx

1 piece of carnelian

7 real pearls (natural or cultured)

A piece of paper and a pen

1 piece of blue fluorite

Next, place seven pearls on a garden wall or in a very sunny window in your home. Make this talisman in the shape of a seven-pointed star, with the top point of the star facing south. This draws on both Bellona's power and the sun's rays. Leave for a week and then carry the pearls with you wherever you go to enhance your courage and seductive power.

With paper and pen, now write the following spell:

Place this in a drawer with the piece of blue fluorite, where it will work every day to bring Bellona's influence so that you have the determination to get your way.

"Bellona, goddess wise,
I take this crystal, blue of hue
And with your blessing I shall be
As strong and wise as you and by necessity
Against all the odds I will be true."

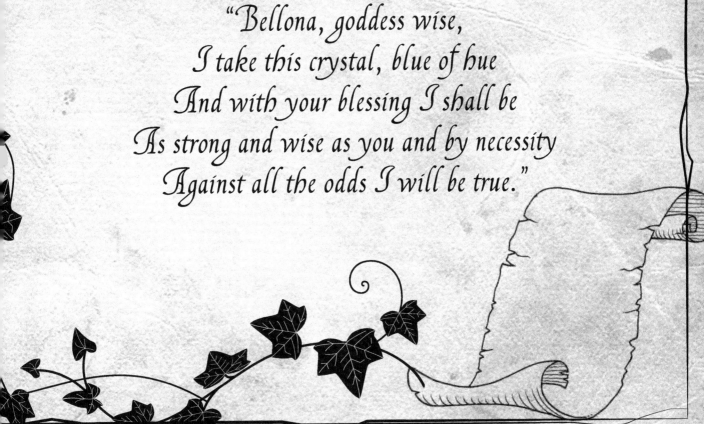

NEW MOON SPELL TO IGNITE PASSION IN SOMEONE'S HEART

This is a traditional European spell to physically attract someone to you, whether it's someone you already know or a stranger in town. Just after the new moon is the perfect time for sending out magical vibrations to create romance, beginnings, growth, and desire. After this spell, it will be a matter of only a few weeks until you see the results you desire.

The day after the new moon, half fill the chalice, goblet, or wineglass with the wine and take a small sip before you begin the spell. Then place it on your altar or table. Thread the ring onto the twine so you can hang it like a pendulum over the chalice. Now say,

"By the power of the moon, this pendulum will ignite passion in 'His/her' (use their name) heart and soul for me."

Hold the pendulum over the glass with your elbow resting on the table. Focus on the ring and relax. It may take a few minutes before the ring starts to swing of its own accord. Be patient, especially if you have never used a pendulum before.

Once it starts to swing, focus your mind on the one you want to desire you and keep saying their name over and over again in your head or out loud. If you don't know their name, imagine their face. If the pendulum swings back and forth or left and right, then your heart's desire is thinking of you now; if the pendulum swings around in a circle, clockwise or counterclockwise, then he/she will think of you tonight.

Now say,

"Moon, sun, and stars bring their love my way.
Let 'him/her' (name) find they want to stay
Each night wrapped close within my arms
Each day infatuated by my charms."

Now take the ring and the thread and wear it around your neck or carry it with you wherever you go. Repeat this spell seven days later and then another seven days later. Within that time your lover should be not only thinking about and lusting after you, but making his or her presence known.

FULL MOON SPELL

ENCHANTMENT FOR LIFESTYLE CHANGE

Estsanatlehi is the Apache and Navajo name for Changing Woman or Turquoise Woman, equivalent to the Great Goddess. She is the consort of Tsohanoai, the sun, and the sister of Yolkai Estsan, the wife of the moon. Her name means "self-renewing one." Whenever she grows old, she walks toward the east until she sees her younger self coming. She then becomes her younger self again. Estsanatlehi lives alone in a floating house on the western waters where the sun, her lover, visits her every night. She is associated with turquoise, rainbows, and mountains.

 his spell must be done on the eve of a full moon and is simply about aligning yourself with the power of the four cardinal directions, so that you can harness Estsanatlehi's powers of renewal from the east.

There are many times in our life when we want to change it, but we are often halted in our tracks by people, emotions, and worries that load us down. This charm works so that you can take that step forward and embrace change.

WHAT YOU WILL NEED

1 large piece of turquoise

Take the piece of turquoise outside on the eve of the full moon and find a space to yourself where you won't be disturbed. First, take the turquoise in one hand and stretch out your arm to the west as if offering it to Estsanatlehi where she lives across the far distant waters. Close your eyes for a moment to relax and calm your mind, then say,

"I embrace change and know it is for the better."

Now turn your body to the north, with hand still outstretched, and repeat the same words, followed by the east and south.

Finally, take the turquoise in both hands and stretch out your arms to the east.

Next chant, *"Sky West and crooked her hair falls East
The flames of change lift Earth to North
From the cauldron Silver burns
And Southward flows her gown of Gold
To track the pathways of the Sun
The Moon and Stars will all be One."*

Bow to the east and then place the turquoise in your pocket or bag.

Finally, thank the goddess:

*"Now I can change my life to whatever I want it to be.
Thank you, Estsanatlehi, for blessing this stone."*

Take the stone with you wherever you go, and change will be your friend forever.

WISH SPELL

This is a simple wish spell that calls on the power of Cancer's element, Water, and its associated correspondences to help you to fulfill a specific wish.

 it calmly at your table or altar, close your eyes, and think about the wish you'd like to come true. Remember, sometimes our wishes are simply that—wishful thinking. Pick the one thing that would make the most difference in your life that is also entirely in the realm of possibility. And remember what you wish for; if you truly believe, it will come true. As most witches say, "Be careful what you wish for!"

WHAT YOU WILL NEED

An athame or knife

1 white candle

A small slip of paper and a pen

1 conch shell or a shell you can close

Now use the athame or knife to carve one or two words into the candle referring to your wish, or any symbols that you might prefer to use.

Next, light the candle and by candlelight, write out your wish in full on the slip of paper, obviously being brief enough to make it fit.

Take the conch shell in your hands, and as you do so, repeat your wish three times, then place the slip of paper inside the shell. Finally drip a few drops of candle wax onto the shell as a symbol of the wish being sealed. Blow out the candle.

Now say,

Finally, bury the conch shell under a tree or bush or place it in a box with a lid somewhere it won't be disturbed. Leave it there for two lunar cycles or until your wish comes true. If your wish doesn't come true within two lunar cycles, then you must repeat the spell again.

"By the power of Water my wish will come true.
By the power of this shell its work will be done.
By the power of this candle my wish will be found.
By the goddess of love and the fire of the sun
Within all that is possible, this wish will be won."

Chapter 8
JULY

Spells and Enchantments for a Happy Home and Family Life

Theme:
Joyful Communication

Plant Energy:
Water Lily for Creative Love

Crystal Power:
Ruby for Peace and Commitment

NAMED BY THE ROMAN SENATE IN HONOR OF THE GREAT GENERAL JULIUS CAESAR, JULY WAS PREVIOUSLY KNOWN AS QUINTILIS. IN ROMAN TIMES, PAGAN FESTIVALS CELEBRATED THE UNTAMED NATURE OF THE LANDSCAPE, THE HOPE FOR MORE RAIN, AND THE AVOIDANCE OF DROUGHT. ALL DEITIES CONCERNED WITH THE WOODS AND WATER WERE APPEASED IN THE DESIRE TO ENCOURAGE THE RIGHT AMOUNT OF RAIN AND A GOOD HARVEST.

or the first three weeks, the sun continues to transit the zodiac sign of Cancer, and from around the 23rd onward it moves through Leo. In Greek mythology, Cancer is linked with the second labor of the mighty hero Hercules when he was assigned the mission of killing the Hydra, a horrible water snake with one hundred heads. In the midst of Hercules' struggle, his enemy, the goddess Hera, ordered a giant crab to go and help the Hydra by digging its claws into Hercules' foot. Howling with pain, the hero stamped on the crab, crushing it to death. Hera, grateful for the crab's attempt to help her, honored it by placing it among the stars as the constellation Cancer.

As a zodiac sign, the energy of Cancer is about family, home, and most of all a sense of belonging. Those born under the sign have a need to "belong" to something, whether a family, clan, or just a big social network. Spells under Cancerian influence are beneficial for home and family life, as well as enabling us to make ourselves "feel at home" in everything we do.

As the sun moves into Leo, the lion, from the dark waters of Cancer, we discover the enflaming energy of Fire. In Egyptian, Mesopotamian, and Greek mythology, the qualities of the lion were associated with rulership and divinity. For many cultures, the symbol of a lion served as a guardian figure, protecting doorways of palaces and temples, and the lion still appears in the rituals of the Chinese New Year.

The magical energy at the end of July is self-concerned and empowering. Magic at this time of year harnesses this regal power to promote your own needs and desires, while still working with the lingering magic of family life. All spell work undertaken at this time of year is about making one's life lucky, golden, and filled with the treasures and love that you know are right for you—not only as an individual but also for your loved ones.

July 3

NATIVE AMERICAN CORN FESTIVAL

LOVE AND HAPPINESS CORN MOTHER POPPET

From now until the end of the summer, the Native American peoples begin to celebrate the coming harvest by giving thanks to the Corn Mother. The Corn Mother is the spirit of the corn, and she represents all that is bountiful and nurturing. Various peoples of the southeastern United States make cornhusk dolls to represent her abundance, placing them in strategic places within the home.

aking your own poppet (a magic wish doll similar to a corn doll) will bring you the love and happiness you want at home. You can either make a poppet by binding bundles of corn together or make one as described below, which also uses the power of magic herbs to maximize the spell's energy.

First, draw a rough shape of a human figure, like a gingerbread man, on a piece of paper. Cut it out and then pin it to your fabric. Cut out from your pattern two fabric gingerbread man shapes and sew them roughly together around the edges, leaving a gap at the top of the head. Write your name on the poppet and the names of your family, as well as the words "Corn Mother."

WHAT YOU WILL NEED

A piece of paper, a pencil, and a pen

Pins, needle, and thread

Natural linen or cotton fabric

Enough dried chamomile flowers, lavender, vervain, rosemary, thyme, and mint to fill your poppet

Cinnamon or cedar incense

A bowl of dried corn kernels or rice

Fill and stuff the poppet with the herbs, then sew up the opening.

Light the incense and hold the poppet in the incense smoke.

As you do so, say,

"Mother Corn,
please bring my home good fortune now.
Bring love and happiness through this charm
To all my family send no harm.
We bless your bounty for all to see
This charm is done,
So mote it be."

Now with the fingers of your other hand, run them through the bowl of corn or rice (which represent the abundance of Earth) and repeat the charm.

Repeat this ritual of holding the poppet in the incense, invoking the Corn Mother with the charm, and then running the fingers of your other hand through the bowl of corn seven times (the number associated with the Corn Mother).

Keep your poppet in a secret place where it won't be disturbed or put it in a powerful place where it will guard the places you work, eat, or play and bring you peaceful days and happy relationships in the home.

THE TANABATA

A SPELL FOR RECONCILIATION AND REUNIONS

The Tanabata is a Japanese star festival, celebrating the long-awaited reunion of the deities Orihime and Hikoboshi, represented by the stars Vega and Altair, respectively. According to legend, the Milky Way separates these lovers, and they are allowed to meet only once a year on the seventh day of the seventh lunar month of the lunar calendar. The date of Tanabata varies by region, but the first festivities usually begin on July 7th of the Gregorian calendar.

WHAT YOU WILL NEED

A pen or a pencil

5 strips of different-colored paper

1 gold-colored chain necklace

1 silver-colored chain necklace

I n present-day Japan, people write their wishes, sometimes as poetry, on small pieces of paper and hang them on bamboo sticks. The bamboo and decorations are often set afloat on a river or burned around midnight or on the next day.

A traditional magical verse (translated into English here) is associated with this festival. It is part of a charm to invoke togetherness and the coming together of all family members. If you are hoping for reconciliation or reunion with family or friends, then this spell is also aligned to bring harmonious meetings in the future months to come.

On each strip of paper, write down one wish that includes some form of happy reunion, reconciliation, or just a better way of relating between you and your loved ones.

Place the gold and silver chains, representing Altair and Vega, respectively, on your table or altar in circle shapes and then place the five wishes in a bundle across the chains.

Now calm your mind and concentrate on the magical ingredients on the table and your wishes.

Then say the following charm:

The following evening, tear up the paper wishes and place the scraps under a tree or bush, or throw them into a stream or river—or anywhere outside where no one can find them—so the magic of the stars, Altair and Vega, may activate your wishes to come true.

"The stars twinkle
On the gold and silver grains of sand.
The five-color paper strips
I have already written.
The stars twinkle,
they watch us from heaven.
Thank you, Altair and Vega, for your blessing."

LUCARIA ROMAN FEAST

CHARM FOR SUCCESSFUL PERSONAL AFFAIRS

The Romans celebrated the Lucaria between July 19th and 21st as the last part of an ancient rite, which had begun back in May to banish all evil spirits from the home. This culminated in the Lucaria's celebration, which was held in a sacred grove and called on all spirits of the woods, forests, and lands for protection in the home and for the coming harvest.

 his spell will protect your home from negativity and give you the energy, self-confidence, and exuberance to attend to your work or career free from family worries.

On the first piece of paper, write the following things about yourself, followed by the words you want to use to end each sentence.

WHAT YOU WILL NEED

2 pieces of paper and a pen

1 silver-colored ring

1 piece of tiger's-eye

A few marigolds or dried marigold leaves

I am really PLEASED when I

- -

I ADORE

- -

I'm FASCINATED by

- -

I ENJOY

- -

I am GRATEFUL for

- -

I WANT

- -

WARM feelings come to me when

- -

I FEEL JOY when

- -

I INTEND to

- -

My PURPOSE is

- -

Fold this up and place it to one side for the moment.

Now take the other piece of paper and draw an imaginary sacred grove. It can be just a circle with symbols to represent trees or spirits, or it can be more elaborate. But whatever comes into your imagination is important, because the power of magic works through our ability to imagine things, and then to believe they will happen.

Now place the silver ring and the tiger's-eye in the center of the "sacred grove" to represent the power of self-confidence and family happiness.

As you do so, say,

Finally, sprinkle some of the marigolds (renowned for their regenerative and protective properties) in all four corners of your home—north, south, east, and west. With the ritual complete, you can now look forward to getting on with your personal mission, and your family or home will be safe from outside influence.

"To the spirits of the sacred grove, let my home and family be blessed with your protection while I carry out all that I must do for myself."

July 20

NEPTUNALIA

A SPELL TO CLEANSE OR CALM THE HOME

Around this date, the Romans appeased and worshipped the god of the seas, Neptune, at a time when there was usually drought or lack of rain. Traditionally, people built huts out of branches and leaves in which they feasted, drank, and made merry. Rituals were performed to purify the home with Neptune's sacred waters. This charm uses the power of Neptune, in addition to Jupiter, Saturn, and Mercury, to calm the energy in your home.

Light the incense and the candle. Stand before your altar or table and take a few moments to feel at one with the energies of your home. Notice perhaps the smells, the sounds, the way the breeze moves the curtains, or how the sunlight enters your room.

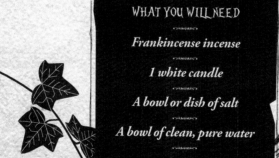

WHAT YOU WILL NEED

Frankincense incense

1 white candle

A bowl or dish of salt

A bowl of clean, pure water

When you are ready, say the following:

*"I charge you Saturn,
Mercury, Jupiter,
Neptune,
To sweep my house clean
of all ill and bane.
This is my will, so mote
it be."*

Take the dish of salt and, working clockwise around the house, throw a pinch of salt into each corner of every room, saying the following:

*"By the powers of Saturn,
I cleanse this house."*

Next, using the same route you used with the salt, take the incense through the house and say,

*"By the powers of
Mercury, I cleanse this
house."*

Do the same with the candle and say,

*"By the powers of
Jupiter, I cleanse this
house."*

Finally, replace the candle on the table and take up the bowl of water. Sprinkle water throughout the house, in every corner and at all exits and entrances, and say,

*"By the powers of
Neptune, I cleanse this
house."*

Set the bowl on the table and stand for a few minutes in silence, and your home will now feel calmer and more peaceful, fresh, and clean. Let the candle burn down until you need to snuff it out, and just before you do so, sprinkle salt on the flames, and then some water, to evoke the powers of all the gods.

July 22

SUN MOVES INTO LEO

RITUAL TO END GOSSIP OR UNKIND BEHAVIOR

This banishing spell invokes the power of the sun as it moves into its favorite zodiac sign, Leo. Leo is about pride, about being sure of yourself, and about not letting others hurt or wound you in any way. With Leo's magic, you can be admired and filled with self-confidence. This spell will also enable you to rid yourself of those who are two-faced, backbiters, or gossipmongers.

 o stop them in their tracks so they leave you alone—without harming them—this spell is based on an old magic ritual used in fifteenth-century England. It was based on the execution of the Duke of Clarence for treason against his brother, King Edward IV. The duke was supposedly drowned, at his request, in a barrel of Malmsey wine! Luckily, you're not going to drown anyone, but you are going "to drown" the bad negativity or antisocial behavior and put an end to it.

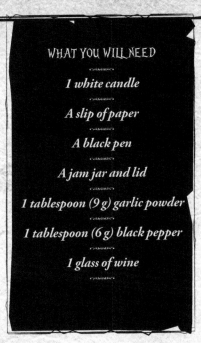

WHAT YOU WILL NEED

1 white candle

A slip of paper

A black pen

A jam jar and lid

1 tablespoon (9 g) garlic powder

1 tablespoon (6 g) black pepper

1 glass of wine

Place the items on your table or altar and light the white candle. With the pen, write on the slip of paper the nature of the antisocial behavior, but not the person's name.

Fold the paper in half and as you do so, say,

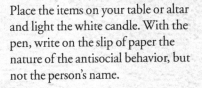

"With this spell I stop your malice.
With this spell I keep my wholeness.
Your reign of power is over and done.
I work this spell with harm to none."

Drop the paper into the jar and add the garlic powder and black pepper to banish negativity. Then pour in the wine to cover the paper. Screw the lid in place and keep the jar by your altar or inside your front door where every time you pass, the magic will be increased threefold. You should start seeing positive results within a couple of weeks.

NEW MOON AND FULL MOON SPELL

A FRIENDSHIP REPAIR CHARM

This spell works in two parts. The first part you must perform just after the new moon, and the second part at the full moon. This will help you to make up with a friend, repair any rift, and get you back together by calling on the goddess Artemis, whose wise counsel as arbitrator was employed by the gods.

WHAT YOU WILL NEED

1 piece of turquoise

1 pink candle

Vanilla extract or essential oil

A piece of paper and a pen

lace the piece of turquoise and the candle at your altar or your table.

Gently rub the vanilla extract on the sides of the candle and then light it.

Ask Artemis to join you by saying,

"With perfumed oil and candle fair
Welcome, Artemis, to this my lair
Where treasured friends can be again
Within one lunar cycle our rift to mend
The bond repaired, the wounds all healed
Our friendship blessed with your appeal."

Sit for a few minutes in quiet contemplation of your friendship and the happy times you had together. When you feel full of love for your pal,

write down all the things you like or admire about your friend. Blow out the candle, fold the paper, and place in a drawer with the piece of turquoise until the evening of the full moon.

On the eve of the full moon, relight the candle, take out the list and the piece of turquoise, and read the list aloud as you hold the turquoise in your hand.

Then say,

"Had I but silver and gold,
I would weave a charm of destiny
For you and I to be entwined
in friendship ever bound.
In this my heart is true and found
The spell now every day be wound
Around our hearts forever.

"With perfumed oil and candle fair
Thank you, Artemis, for this day true
Where treasured friends can be again
By my side within day one.
The bond repaired, the wounds all healed
Our friendship blessed with your appeal."

Bow to the candle, then gently blow it out as if blowing a kiss to your friend. Arrange to meet your friend and take the turquoise with you to present as a magical peace offering.

HAPPY HOME GOOD LUCK ENCHANTMENT

This general spell, to be cast anytime during the month, will bring you beneficial energy in and around the home, as well as improve relationships with family members. But apart from peace and harmony in the home, we would all like a bit of luck now and again, too. This enchantment calls on the three Graces: Aglaea (Splendor), Euphrosyne (Mirth), and Thalia (Good Cheer). Three was an important number in ancient Greek magical texts, and the triple goddess in the guise of the Graces was frequently invoked. With the help of these graceful, enchanting goddesses, you too can make your home a lucky place to live.

The twelve magic ingredients used in this spell represent the twelve astrological signs and invoke the attributes of the powers of the three Graces. Aglaea is the cardinal virtue, and her signs are Aries, Cancer, Libra, and Capricorn; Euphrosyne is the fixed virtue, and her signs are Taurus, Leo, Scorpio, and Aquarius; Thalia is mutable, and her signs are Gemini, Virgo, Sagittarius, and Pisces.

WHAT YOU WILL NEED

3 yellow rosebuds (or 3 images of yellow rosebuds)

3 garlic cloves

3 gold-colored coins

3 gold-colored rings

A small bag or pouch

Gold ribbon

1 iron nail

Place the rosebuds, garlic, coins, and rings in the bag and tie it up with the gold ribbon. Take the bag and walk around your home in a clockwise direction, starting at the outer perimeter and holding the bag in front of you. Cover every part of your home and gradually work your way into a center point. As you walk, repeat the following charm,

"Thrice times I walk to honor my home.
Three Graces help me wherever I roam
To bring me luck in all I do
My family too, with help from you."

Now make the same walk, but in a counterclockwise direction, repeating the charm below:

"This magic pouch holds virtues sweet
Each zodiac sign, each element writ
With love and luck sealed in its place
It's time to thank you all for Grace."

Finally take your pouch and hang it over your front door using an iron nail, which has the magical property of fixing all that you desire in place in the home. Your home will be blessed with luck for months to come.

Chapter 9
AUGUST
Spells and Enchantments for Creativity, Self-Promotion, and Persuasion

Theme:
Creativity

Plant Energy:
Cedar for Liberation

Crystal Power:
Peridot for Insight and Wisdom

WITH THE SUMMER HARVEST FESTIVALS BEGINNING IN THE NORTHERN HEMISPHERE, AUGUST IS TRADITIONALLY A MONTH OF ABUNDANCE, COMMUNITY SPIRIT, AND CREATIVE ENERGY. SOME HISTORIANS BELIEVE IT WAS RENAMED AUGUST IN HONOR OF EMPEROR AUGUSTUS, BECAUSE IT WAS THE TIME OF SEVERAL OF HIS GREAT TRIUMPHS, INCLUDING THE CONQUEST OF EGYPT. OTHER SCHOLARS CLAIM THE NAME DERIVES FROM THE "AUGURS," THE ORACULAR PRIESTS WHO INTERPRETED THE WILL OF THE GODS AND PREDICTED EVENTS BY OBSERVING THE FLIGHTS OF BIRDS. IN AUGUST, BIRDS BEGIN TO STIR FROM THEIR NESTING GROUNDS AND PREPARE FOR THEIR AUTUMN MIGRATORY.

uring the first few weeks of August, the sun is still moving through the fiery flames of Leo. The pagan festival of Lammas signifies the end of the summer and the beginning of the harvest season. Spells were cast in the hope of a bountiful harvest, and it was timely to—quite literally—make hay and make love while the sun shone. As the sun crosses the cusp of Virgo (the Virgin) around the 22nd, there is a different energy in the air. This energy is about quick thinking, attention to detail, and purity of thought and mind. Spells are cast to enhance one's own attributes, to persuade others of your plans, to advance your ideas, and to get quick results. Virgo magic is precise, measured, and specific.

One Greek myth identifies Virgo with Erigone, the daughter of Icarius of Athens. Icarius was made a grape farmer and winemaker by Dionysus. But his wine was so strong that some of those who drank it lay in a stupor and appeared dead. A group of shepherds avenged their supposedly poisoned friends by killing Icarius. Icarius's dog, Maera, brought Erigone to her father's body, whereupon both she and the dog committed suicide. Zeus then chose to honor all three by placing them in the sky as constellations: Icarius as Boötes, Erigone as Virgo, and Maera as either Canis Major or Canis Minor. This tale is an analogy for our own ability to "read between the lines" to see the truth of the matter, not just what we see before us like the crazed shepherds; and like Erigone's, the Virgo mind is pure, untainted, and loyal. This energy therefore allows you to think before you act and stand firm in your choices.

As August comes to a close, so too do holiday makers return to their homes, and schools and universities start again. This is a great time for crafting spells that will enable you to succeed in your studies or to help others start new ventures. The magic crystals associated with Virgo, such as peridot and moss agate, can be added to any spell to double its power and bring you benefits more quickly.

LUGHNASADH SABBAT

A SPELL TO EMPOWER YOU WITH CREATIVE WISDOM

Also known as Lammas, this traditional Celtic celebration marks the beginning of the end of summer in the northern hemisphere, as well as the coming harvest. It is the day to celebrate mother earth and the abundance in nature. The Sabbat is about the cycle of birth, life, death, and rebirth when the Grain God dies, to be reborn in the spring. This is the day to call on the Great Goddess to nurture all aspects of our own creativity, whether physical, mental, or artistic at home, at work, or in art. This spell will empower you with creative confidence in all that you intend to do. If you feel the need to finalize something in your life or "wrap up" unfinished business, this charm will also enable you to do so.

WHAT YOU WILL NEED

1 small piece of obsidian

5 small pieces of peridot

1 red candle

 Hold the piece of obsidian between both hands close to your chest and repeat the following blessing:

"With this stone I will grow in creative power
To become at one with the universe.
Thank you, Great Goddess, for blessing me with strength."

Now place the stone in an east corner of your home to promote and strengthen all affairs surrounding your own coming harvest of creativity.

On your altar or table, arrange five pieces of peridot (to enhance your powers or insight) in the pattern of the magic symbol Cauda Draconis, known as the dragon's tail, as shown on page 16. Five is the number of creativity, so for five evenings in a row, sit beside your altar, light the red candle, and gaze into the candle flame. Take each piece of peridot in turn in your hands and, holding each one close to your chest, repeat the following spell:

" God of Grain begone from sight.
It's time to harvest seeds of light.
Let Mother Earth bring ears of corn
That hear my thoughts and sound the horn.
Let Mother Earth bring fruitful pies
That I can eat to be so wise."

After one week, turn each stone 360 degrees clockwise once. After the second week, turn the stones back 360 degrees counterclockwise. As you do, repeat the spell above and then add:

"Bless you, Mother Earth, Great Goddess, for the forthcoming creative harvest that I can now reap."

From now on, you can expect great thoughts, inspired meetings, new contacts, and abundant opportunities.

GHOST FESTIVAL

SPELL TO VITALIZE PERSONAL POWER

Around this time, traditional Chinese folk celebrate the dead, including their ancestors believed to return to the world as ghosts. Ritualistic food offerings are made to welcome the dead. Incense is burned, and elaborate gifts such as clothes, gold, and other fine goods are prepared for the visiting spirits. Feasts would be served for the family celebration, with empty seats specially prepared for each of the deceased. This spell uses ingredients that invoke the help of your own friendly ancestors.

 Place all your ingredients on the table or altar beside you, then cast an imaginary magic circle around you as explained on page 78.

As you cast the circle, say,

"I invite all spirits and energies to remain who are happy and a good influence to me. I banish all those energies and spirits who are negative and ask you to depart now."

Now take up the bell and ring it five times to welcome the good spirits of your ancestors.

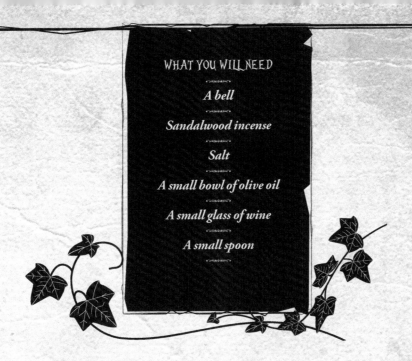

WHAT YOU WILL NEED

A bell

Sandalwood incense

Salt

A small bowl of olive oil

A small glass of wine

A small spoon

As you do, say,

> *"All spirits and ancestors*
> *that love me truly,*
> *be welcomed here,*
> *so mote it be."*

Now light the incense and sprinkle salt into the bowl of oil while you say,

> *"By the elements and*
> *ancestral spirits, I purify*
> *and vitalize myself."*

Now pour the glass of wine into the bowl, gently stir your alchemical mixture with the spoon as you close your eyes, and say,

> *"By alchemy,*
> *by spirits true*
> *My ancestors now*
> *come to me*
> *To always help*
> *and give resolve*
> *To empower my world*
> *and bring me love."*

Finally, thank your ancestors:

> *"Thank you, all spirits*
> *and ancestors, the spell*
> *is done, now return with*
> *love, and all be gone."*

Leave the magic potion for one night and then pour it away in the morning, and your whole being will be empowered with fresh vitality.

KAMALA HINDU GODDESS

INVOCATION FOR CREATIVE SKILLS

The Hindu goddess Lakshmi was known in one of her incarnations as Kamala, the goddess of wealth and creativity. As the goddess of material beauty, she could be invoked to bring creative skills and was given offerings of rice and ghee, a kind of butter. Drawing on her powers can bestow you with creative skill so that you too can fill your life with pleasure and wealth of every kind.

WHAT YOU WILL NEED

5 white candles

A small bowl of rice

ight the five candles and place them in a circle on your altar or table to form the five points of a pentagram shape.

Place the bowl of rice before you, and one by one take grains of rice and place them on the altar in a circle about the size of a dinner plate. As you pick up a grain of rice and place it down, repeat the following spell until you have completed your rice circle:

"Kamala, bring me creative skill in work and play
For everlasting wealth in every day.
For art or craft, for thoughts or deeds
For success and health, and other needs
For pleasure, joy, and greater times
Let creativity be the guide to make life mine."

Once the spell is complete, take each grain of rice from the table and place it back in the bowl, one at a time. Repeat the spell again, and when you have finally replaced all the grains, thank the goddess by saying,

"Kamala, I give thanks
to your divine power
To allow me to give grace
to all creative enterprises,
so mote it be."

Sit for a few minutes in relaxed silence by closing your eyes and thinking about your creative skill or the things you would like to be creative with. Then blow out the candles. To honor Kamala, scatter the rice in a river, stream, or lake.

SUN MOVES INTO VIRGO

ENCHANTMENT TO SELL YOUR IDEAS

Around this date, the sun moves into precise and efficient Virgo, enabling us to cast spells that are progressive, shrewd, and insightful. With the help of runes—the powerful Norse symbols that are used as oracles and for invoking the power of the gods—you can sell yourself and your ideas, market your wares, or become so charismatic that you could sell ice to an Eskimo.

On your table or altar, draw or paint the following runic symbols (page 143) on the seven smooth pebbles:

The rune Ansuz will bring you wisdom. Hagalaz will activate the spell. Jera will help prove your value and worth. Dagaz brings positive transformation. Mannaz is for perfect communication. Wunjo is the rune of joy and ensures that the results of the spell will be a positive influence over others. Inguz allows the spell to last forever and prevents negative influence.

Light the candles, place them in a circle, and then take each stone in your hand one at a time and say,

"Bless you, gods of the runes, for my future success."

Place each stone beside a candle. When all are in place, walk around the table in a clockwise direction seven times (the number of runic magic).

WHAT YOU WILL NEED

7 smooth round pebbles or stones

Indelible pen or paint to mark the rune symbols on the stones

7 white tea light candles

A small box with a lid

Finally, place the stones in a box and say the following to invoke the power of the gods:

"Ansuz, Laguz, gods of old
Let my powers of persuasion
begin to unfold
That all that I say,
write, or desire
Will bring me the dreams to
which I aspire
That others will hear me,
amazed and impressed
And my ideas will sell, for
this I am blessed."

Place the box in a safe place, preferably in a room or office where you work or do most of your business. (If you ever need to recharge your persuasive selling powers, take the stones out of the box and hold each of them for a few minutes while repeating the preceeding spell.)

Let the tea lights extinguish on their own before you place the box in its special place.

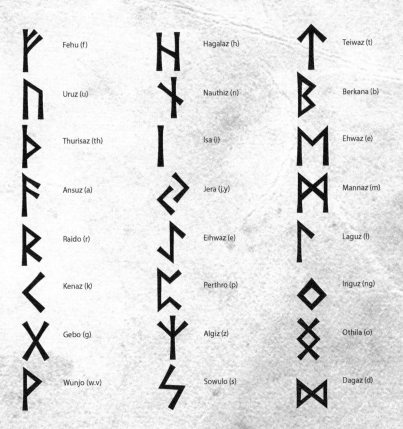

Fehu (f)

Uruz (u)

Thurisaz (th)

Ansuz (a)

Raido (r)

Kenaz (k)

Gebo (g)

Wunjo (w.v)

Hagalaz (h)

Nauthiz (n)

Isa (i)

Jera (j,y)

Eihwaz (e)

Perthro (p)

Algiz (z)

Sowulo (s)

Teiwaz (t)

Berkana (b)

Ehwaz (e)

Mannaz (m)

Laguz (l)

Inguz (ng)

Othila (o)

Dagaz (d)

August 26

OPS FESTIVAL

SUCCESS AND PROSPERITY SPELL

This is an ancient talismanic spell from the French Renaissance, allegedly used by a white witch who called on the power of Ops, the goddess of abundance, to help Guillaume Budé, an idle scholar, rise to fame as head librarian for King Francis I of France and write a highly esteemed treatise on ancient coins.

 or your own privileged future, cast this spell in the evening between 6 p.m. and 9 p.m., which are the goddess's most precious hours when she gave a silver coin to any lost child or beggar in the street.

First, place a small dish on the drawing of the pentacle on your altar or table and put in the cinnamon stick and the three coins. Just before you put each coin in the dish, tap it seven times with the wand as you say,

"Oh magical Ops, your silver coin of the moon,
Shine bright for us all, and bring me wealth soon.
Bring coins to my hands and tenfold grow strong,
Then tenfold again until tenfold be done."

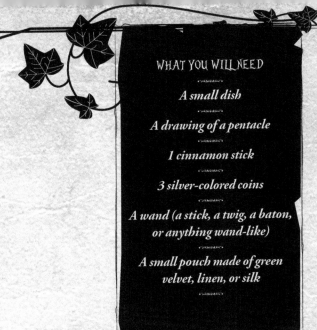

WHAT YOU WILL NEED

A small dish

A drawing of a pentacle

1 cinnamon stick

3 silver-colored coins

A wand (a stick, a twig, a baton,
or anything wand-like)

A small pouch made of green
velvet, linen, or silk

Now with your wand, "stir" the air
above the dish in a clockwise direction
seven times and say,

" *Fire, Earth, Water, Air, essence of light,*
Antimony, vitriol, share treasure this night.
Share with me riches of silver and gold.
Success and prosperity, all will be shown. "

Now close your eyes for a few
moments to let the beneficial energy
come to you through the magic
talisman. Put the coins and the
cinnamon in the pouch and leave it
somewhere safe overnight in
the moonlight.

For the next lunar cycle (four weeks),
either carry the bag with you or keep
it near your bed where you will see
it every night and know that it is
working its magic for you.

NEW MOON SPELL

A SPELL TO DRAW MONEY TO YOU

We would all like to have a little more cash flowing through our fingers. This medieval spell calls on the elemental spirits just after a new moon, when their powers will help you to attract to you what you truly need.

During the first few days just after a new moon, rub a white candle with patchouli oil, then light it and place it on a table or your altar.

Gaze at the candle flame, relax, and think of money being drawn to you. Now put the coin in front of the candle, followed by the four malachite stones (for financial gain) around the candle and coin.

Now say,

" By the power of Air, Fire, Water, Earth
Let money come to me by good deeds done.
Let such be given generously, but harm come to none,
Multiply this coin, blessed spirits, for all my worth
So mote it be. "

Sit quietly for a few more minutes while you gaze at the flame and try to imagine the money you truly need, rather than just want. Blow out the candle and carry the coin and the malachite stones with you in a pouch to maximize the rewards that are coming your way.

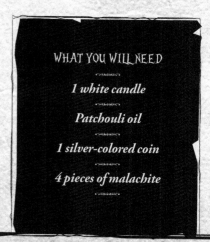

WHAT YOU WILL NEED

1 white candle

Patchouli oil

1 silver-colored coin

4 pieces of malachite

FULL MOON SPELL

This full moon spell will help you with all forms of successful negotiations, particularly when you want to find compromise or be in harmony with others.

or this ritual, you will need a black piece of paper and a white crayon. Drawing the magic symbol in white strengthens its power. Attach the white symbol to your mirror and every time you look at yourself, meditate for a few moments and imagine success pouring into a goblet. Beneficial influences and useful contacts will soon appear for your negotiation.

Bury seven pieces of white quartz crystal in the ground in the symbol shape of Albus (or if you don't have access to a yard, place the pattern on the floor where it won't be disturbed). Sprinkle some sage leaves over the area for blessing and harmony and to protect it from negative energy. Walk around the pattern in a clockwise direction every day for seven days, repeating the mantra

"Harmony and negotiation will bring me justice and peace."

By the next full moon, you will be able to negotiate anything.

WHAT YOU WILL NEED

A piece of black paper

A white pen or crayon

The magic symbol for Albus (page 16)

7 small pieces or shards of white quartz crystal

Sage leaves, fresh or dried

SUCCESS SPELL

A SPELL TO DRAW MONEY TO YOU

Drawing on the power of the sun and moon, corresponding to gold and silver respectively, this is a simple spell to gain success in everything you intend to do in the next two weeks.

 lace a red candle on one side of your room, and on the other side, place a white candle.

First, light the red candle, then take the two rings in your right hand and pick up the red candle with your left hand. Walk in a straight line across the room directly to the white candle, and using the red one, light it. Set down the candles so they are side by side.

Now say,

*"Sun with red and moon with white
Take this charm and make it right
So I may walk forth without doubt and fear,
As skies of success draw ever near."*

Lay the two rings in front of the candles. (The gold ring in front of the white candle and the silver ring in front of the red candle will balance the magic ingredients.) Wait for the candles to burn halfway down and then take the two rings wherever you wish success to follow you.

For example, when you walk through the door for a job interview or anywhere you need success, remember how you walked in a straight line from the red candle to the white candle. Do the same as you make your way through the world to success.

WHAT YOU WILL NEED

1 red candle

1 white candle

1 gold-colored ring

1 silver-colored ring

FINANCIAL STABILITY SPELL

The magical number six and the geomantic sigil Carcer are both symbolic of strength, willpower, and stability. By drawing on the power of this magical combination, you can look forward to a more stable financial future.

Place six white quartz crystals, symbolizing confident decision making, in the shape of the Carcer symbol (page 16) on a table, with a piece of black tourmaline in the middle (to enhance all material gain). For six days, move each of the quartz crystals one place forward to the next position in a counterclockwise direction. Then repeat the process for six days in a clockwise direction.

Each time you move a stone, say,

" Thank you Earth, and all the Stars
For this my state be True
That I can feel safe, endowed
With Wealth, in all I say and do. "

This will now activate the magic to make you feel empowered and ready to make your life more stable.

After twelve days of moving the crystals, place six pieces of amethyst (for progress) in a circle on your altar. Each day for six more days, place one of the white quartz stones alongside the amethysts, and finally place the black tourmaline in the center. This magic ritual will gradually bring you wealth and security and enhance financial, material, and family stability.

WHAT YOU WILL NEED

6 white quartz crystals

1 piece of black tourmaline

6 pieces of amethyst

Chapter 10
SEPTEMBER

Spells and Enchantments for Personal Growth

Theme:
Adaptability

Plant Energy:
Willow Tree for Equality

Crystal Power:
Sapphire for Good Fortune

SEPTEMBER IS NAMED AFTER THE LATIN WORD FOR SEVEN, *SEPTEM*, BECAUSE IT WAS THE SEVENTH MONTH OF THE YEAR IN THE OLD ROMAN CALENDAR. UNTIL THE ROMANS INVADED NORTHERN EUROPE, THE ANGLO-SAXONS HAD NAMED THE MONTH "GERST MONATH," BARLEY MONTH, OR "HAEFEST MONATH," HARVEST MONTH, BOTH REFERRING TO THE HARVESTING OF BARLEY GRAIN, WHICH THEY MADE INTO THEIR FAVORITE ALCOHOLIC DRINK. IN THE NORTHERN HEMISPHERE, SEPTEMBER IS USUALLY ASSOCIATED WITH HARVESTS AND THE COMING AUTUMN, WHILE IN THE SOUTHERN HEMISPHERE, IT IS ASSOCIATED WITH THE COMING SPRING. THE EQUINOX ON THE 21ST MARKS THE SUN'S THIRD IMPORTANT POINT IN ITS JOURNEY AROUND THE ZODIAC, AND ITS MOVE FROM THE SIGN OF VIRGO INTO LIBRA.

he first three weeks of September are still energized by the sun in Virgo. Spells to do with personal achievement and the finalization of tasks or projects are favored. People are more willing to make contact, offer up new ideas, or point out mistakes without judgment. Virgo energy is also about keeping fit and looking after oneself—in mind, body, and spirit—and as the sun approaches the cusp of Libra, there is a realization that all the effort you put into your work will soon pay off.

As the sun moves into Libra on or around the 21st, the energy changes to a more romantic, light-hearted one. In Babylonian astrology, the constellation of Libra was known as the "scales" as well as the "claws of the Scorpio," which it took from its neighboring constellation. The scales were held sacred to the sun god Shamash, who was the god of truth and justice, and today the zodiac sign of Libra is also concerned with fairness, truth, and equality in relationships. It has also been suggested that the scales are an allusion to the equinox marking a twenty-four-hour period when day and night are equal in length.

Saint Michael the Archangel's Day falls on the 29th to mark the end of Lammas, the harvest season which began August 1st. It is believed in England that picking blackberries from the hedgerows after this date is unlucky because when Michael threw Lucifer out of heaven, he landed in a bramble bush and tainted the plant with evil power from that day. For the Romans, Vulcan, the god of volcanoes and earthquakes, ruled September; these natural upheavals from the core of the earth were more frequent around this time of year in the eastern Mediterranean, marking this as the month of volatile energy, courage, and purpose. September is therefore a time to not only work on yourself, but to respect the passion of others.

FEAST OF DURGA

AN ENCHANTMENT TO BE MORE SELF-SUFFICIENT

At some point between the 5th and 17th of September, the Hindus begin their nine-day-long celebration to honor the mother goddess, Durga. Durga means "invincible," and her legend tells of her great battle with the demon Mahishasura, who shape-shifted into buffalo, lion, elephant, and buffalo again before being beheaded by Durga's trident.

Durga's attributes are silver and gold, and in some regions of India she is invoked to encourage wealth and self-sufficiency into the family. With her help, you can overcome the demons of poverty and see a way forward to making your future more secure.

On your table or altar, make a magic circle with the candles by placing the four green candles at each cardinal point (north, south, east, west) and the white candle in the center. Put the bay leaves, fluorite stones, and the coins into the bowl and place this to the right of the circle.

Place your photo in front of the candles.

Light the white candle in the middle and then the four green candles. Now take up your photo and gaze at your image while you concentrate in your mind on what wealth and security mean to you, just for a minute.

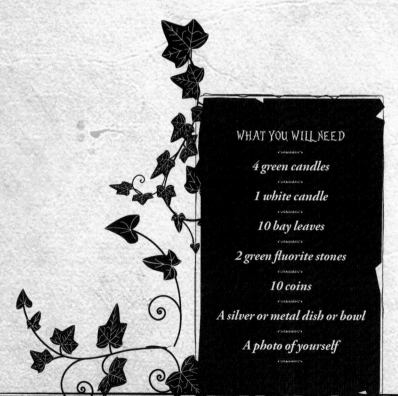

WHAT YOU WILL NEED

4 green candles

1 white candle

10 bay leaves

2 green fluorite stones

10 coins

A silver or metal dish or bowl

A photo of yourself

Next, still looking at your image, say this charm five times to invoke the magic number of the circle and Durga's powers:

" Security is coming soon to me,
Wealth is flowing unto me,
The power of self-reliance for all to see,
Durga, great goddess, send to me,
Let it come, so mote it be."

Now sit for a few minutes and visualize opportunities coming to you to increase your income, or how you could have all you need to be happy. The longer you can hold this happy image in your mind, the better. Once you feel in an empowered state of mind, replace the photo, blow out the candles, and place the silver bowl of magic ingredients before you.

Run your fingers through the bay leaves and fluorite stones in the bowl to stir up their magical powers to bring you wealth.

Next, take the coins from the bowl and scatter them randomly on the floor in a corner or part of your room where they won't be disturbed for three lunar cycles. As you scatter them, say,

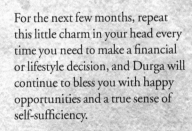

" Scatter money on the floor
Happiness comes back through the door.
Thank you, Durga, for your charm
From now on to us comes no harm."

For the next few months, repeat this little charm in your head every time you need to make a financial or lifestyle decision, and Durga will continue to bless you with happy opportunities and a true sense of self-sufficiency.

DAY OF RHIANNON

BRING TO LIFE YOUR INNER MAGIC

Rhiannon was a mystical, magical lady of Welsh legends who rode a white stallion and was desired by a Welsh prince who could never catch up with her even though she rode slowly, luring him on. Though she was invoked for love spells in medieval times, this love spell is meant to give self-value and self-worth to you, and you alone.

This enchantment is about bringing to life your own inner magic, which often we neglect at the expense of doing magical work "outside" of ourselves. By drawing on the magical powers within, which are located in your aura or subtle body energy, you can then connect to the magical energy of the otherworld. This spell works to bring you in alignment with the balance of magic in nature and the spiritual world, to use these powers for good purposes.

Sit in a quiet place, preferably cross-legged with your back straight. Relax, close your eyes, and calm your mind by breathing slowly and counting down each in-breath from twenty to one.

WHAT YOU WILL NEED

You

Once you're relaxed, put your hands together so the ends of the fingers of each hand touch each other and hold about 5 inches (12.5 cm) or so away from your chest. Now gradually move your hands in the same, almost-touching position down to a point just below your belly button. You should sense a change in energy through your hands.

This point just below your belly button is called the hara and is the point in your body often referred to as the center of power, the place where you are connected to the spiritual or supernatural realms.

Now stand up, facing the east, and with your arms spread wide and the palms of your hands upward, say,

"All that is One,
All that is the universe within and without,
Eternal and infinite,
Let me be in touch with the true life force that is mine
That I may love myself and trust in my instincts
And to know that as a child of the universe,
Like Rhiannon, I have the power of magic too."

Now move your hands from the top of your head gradually down to your toes in a sweeping motion.

Raise your arms again to the sky and visualize the universal energy being drawn in and down to your magical power center. Take your time and don't rush; just enjoy the feeling of welcoming the universal magic to link to your inner being. Repeat the chant three times.

Finally, place your hands with fingers touching each other just hovering over your hara spot and feel the sizzling energy of your connection to the universe. Not only will this spell enhance your innate magical force, but you will realize that you can love yourself because you love the universe and everything in it.

AUTUMN EQUINOX

SELF-EMPOWERMENT CHARM

As day and night are equal again, just for one day,
this is a time for a complete focus on your own inner
balance. This ancient spell from a medieval grimoire will
empower you with inspirational energy, making you
ready to move forward into the next season of the year,
invigorated and ready for action.

WHAT YOU WILL NEED

7 pieces of beryl

1 red candle

7 pieces of obsidian

*A cardboard box with a lid
(optional)*

ay the seven pieces of beryl, which bestow sharp thinking and clarity, on your altar or table in the pattern of the magic symbol Rubeus (page 16). This is a potent symbol of power, assigned by Cornelius Agrippa to the zodiac sign of Scorpio, the sign of personal power.

In the gap between the top two crystals of the symbol layout, place the red candle, representing passion. It will invoke zestful fire energy.

Light the candle and repeat this affirmation seven times:

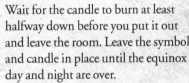

"I will rediscover my own power and will believe in my own light."

Wait for the candle to burn at least halfway down before you put it out and leave the room. Leave the symbol and candle in place until the equinox day and night are over.

The following day, place seven pieces of obsidian (for self-confidence) in the Rubeus symbol pattern in the cardboard box or bury it in the garden with the top of the symbol pointing north to activate the power of the element Water. Leave for two full moon cycles to maximize personal power, then remove the stones and keep them in a safe place.

SUN MOVES INTO LIBRA

ENCHANTMENT TO EMPOWER RELATIONSHIPS

As the sun moves into Libra around this day, we are thrown into the airy delights of love relationships. The goddess of Fire in Lithuanian mythology, Gabija, was worshipped by offering bread and salt and invoked to empower lovers with renewed passion. This spell will empower any love relationship with fiery energy.

 ight the incense, then pass the pink tourmaline through the smoke. As you do so, repeat the following words:

" Gabija, goddess of fire,
Light the way to our
heart's desire
Of golden sun,
and lovers' power
Light the way,
fill my bower
With potent magic,
pure and true
And with this spell,
be happy too."

WHAT YOU WILL NEED

Frankincense incense

1 piece of pink tourmaline

Cedar oil or cedar leaves

5 red candles

5 pink candles

A chalice filled with natural spring water

Place the tourmaline crystal on your table or altar and sprinkle a little cedar oil or a few leaves over the crystal.

Place the red candles in a tight circle first, followed by the pink candles surrounding the red ones. Light the candles. Make sure all candles are lit before repeating the following.

Take the crystal in your hand and stretch it out toward the direction south and say,

"Element of Fire,
pure and strong,
Bring us strength to
mend all wrongs."

Now to the north say,

"Element of Earth,
deep and clean,
Bring us power to
manifest a dream."

Now to the west say,

"Element of Water,
forever flowing,
Bring us love and
passion growing."

Now to the east say,

"Element of Air,
oh wise and true,
Bring us wisdom in
all we do."

Next, take one of the pink candles, hold it out toward the south, and say,

"Spirit of the South,
let the goddess shine her
light through you."

Hold the candle to the north and say,

"Spirit of the North,
let the goddess send her
power through you."

Hold the candle to the east and say,

"Spirit of the East,
let the goddess say her
words through you."

Finally, hold the candle to the west and say,

"Spirit of the West,
let the goddess show her
love through you."

Replace the candle and take up the crystal. Place the crystal in the chalice of water and leave it for one day and one night for the magic to work.

Thank the goddess Gabija for her presence and her help, then blow out the candles.

After you have left the crystal for one day and one night, remove it from the chalice and place it in a window where it can receive maximum sunlight during the day to continue to empower your love relationships.

September 26

FEAST OF SAINT MICHAEL

ANGEL SPELL TO TAKE CHARGE OF YOUR LIFE

Michael, the warrior saint, was an archangel who defeated all evil and was later believed to empower those who honored him with spiritual protection. On his feast day, you can call on him to help you overcome all the demons of self-doubt, stress, emotional tension, and negative thoughts and replace them with dedication to yourself, by going with the flow rather than resisting it, and taking control of your life.

WHAT YOU WILL NEED

A piece of paper

A pen

2 glasses of red wine

A cauldron or cooking pot

1 teaspoon cardamom

1 teaspoon cinnamon

5 cloves

A spoon

he magic ingredients of spiced, or mulled, wine were often used in seventeenth-century grimoires to call on the angels, who, according to one legend, used to take a sip of the potion before returning to their heavenly domain!

On a piece of paper, draw a circle and then a square around the outside of the circle. In each of the four corners of the square, write the name of Michael and in the center of the circle write your name.

Pour the red wine into your cauldron or cooking pot and heat gently until simmering, then add the spices and the paper. Let the brew simmer for a few more minutes, then turn off the heat and leave for one hour to cool down. During the hour, write down all the things you want in your life, or those things you long to do or be: to be a better mother or lover; to be empowered with self-belief or abundance; to attract good energy to you; or to be able to be in charge of your feelings rather than allowing your feelings to control you.

Most important, exactly seven minutes before the end of the hour (traditionally, angel magic begins at seven minutes to the hour), stir the cauldron and repeat the following:

Bring the mixture to a boil and then turn off the heat.

Spoon a little of the liquid into a glass, and when cool, take a small sip to honor Michael and mark the beginning of the new self-empowered you.

> "*Archangel Michael, send out your strength*
> *So that I too can attract goodness into my life.*
> *With this potion stirred once it will be done*
> *This potion stirred twice all evil be gone*
> *This potion stirred thrice my life be fun*
> *This potion stirred last, my empowerment begin.*"

NEW MOON SPELL

WRITE YOUR MAGIC WISH LIST AND IT WILL COME TRUE

Thoth was the Egyptian god of the moon, wisdom, writing, astrology, botany, mathematics, theology, and all knowledge, human or divine. It is his knowledge that will come through you as you write your magical wish list on the day or evening of the new moon. This is a time of seeding and conception, the moment before a flash of insight or breakthrough, the end of a cycle, and the beginning of a new one.

 ight a white candle to harness the power of the new moon and sit comfortably at a table.

First, write down the following spell:

"With this pen
I so inscribe
Desires and wishes
as described,
Bring me, Thoth,
all that I think
And secure my future
with this ink."

Now start to write your wish list, and as you do so, say aloud each wish three times. You can have no more than seven wishes, the magical number of Thoth.

Once you have finished writing, fold the paper, place it in the envelope, and seal it. Now carefully drip a few drops of wax from the candle onto the envelope to bless and seal it with the power of Thoth and to make your wishes come true.

Always be careful what you wish for, because it will manifest before you know it.

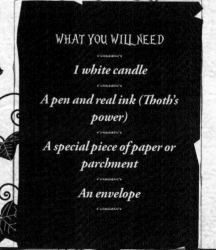

WHAT YOU WILL NEED

1 white candle

A pen and real ink (Thoth's power)

A special piece of paper or parchment

An envelope

FULL MOON SPELL

A SPELL FOR MANIFESTING AN ASPIRATION

This full moon spell will help you with all forms of successful negotiations, particularly when you want to find compromise or be in harmony with others.

rape the white cloth outside on a wall, garden seat, or in a tree—it must be raised above the ground for the spell to work. Place a piece of tiger's-eye (symbolizing fiery intentions and willpower) on the cloth.

Take a handful of fresh or dried basil and scatter gently over the cloth. Basil is the herb of protection and anoints the charm with protective qualities.

For a few moments, close your eyes and repeat your aspiration or desire over and over again.

Next, hold the tiger's-eye, still in the cloth, in your hand, while you vigorously shake the basil leaves to the ground. As you do so, repeat the spell:

Write this affirmation on a piece of paper and tuck it away in a secret place with the cloth and tiger's-eye, and by the next waxing moon your dream will manifest.

"I am of the Universe, I flow with the cosmic sea, and wherever it will take me now, will lead me to manifest my aspiration."

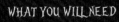

WHAT YOU WILL NEED

1 piece of white natural-fiber cloth (linen or cotton), about 1 square foot (30 square cm)

1 piece of tiger's-eye

Fresh or dried basil leaves

A piece of paper and a pen

BLESSING THE HOME SPELL

The early Carmelite monks were Christian hermits who lived on Mount Carmel in the Holy Land during the late Middle Ages. They built a chapel dedicated to the Blessed Virgin, who they called the Lady of the Place. Whatever spiritual practice you follow or believe, the Lady of Carmel will bring balance of mind, spirit, and soul to your home and family.

WHAT YOU WILL NEED

Sandalwood incense or a smudging stick of white sage

A small piece of paper

A pen and black ink

A small pouch or bag made of black velvet or silk

1 small white quartz crystal

1 pinch of dried sage

1 pinch of dried wormwood

1 silver-colored coin

1 strand of your hair

1 piece of raffia or twine

 irst, repeat the following psychic healing affirmations five times.

1. *My spiritual self will stay with me even when I am being pragmatic.*
2. *Love is all around me; I know it is there to benefit me.*
3. *I believe in the life force that heals all.*
4. *The power of belief is mine to give to others and to myself.*

When you are ready, use a small bundle of dried white sage or a sandalwood incense stick to "smudge" or cleanse negative energy from your home. Light the sage or incense, walk from room to room, and ensure that the wafting smoke or incense fills the room. Take your time and don't rush.

In each room repeat out loud,

"All negative energy be gone, all negative energy be gone, thank you, Lady of the Place."

Once you have performed this part of the ritual, do the following:

Draw a pentagram (page 15) in black ink on a small piece of paper. Roll the paper and place it in the black pouch or bag.

Also place in the pouch the white quartz crystal (Fire energy), pinch of sage (Air energy), pinch of wormwood (Earth energy), silver coin (Water energy), and strand of your hair.

Tie the bag up with some raffia or twine using three knots. As you tie each knot, say the following:

*"As My Lady's spell is done
So my home be ever loved
My spirit self in harmony
With all I do or think or be."*

Then place the knotted pouch on a window ledge for one lunar cycle to ensure spiritual, mental, and emotional harmony.

Chapter 11
OCTOBER

Spells and Enchantments for Love Relationships

Theme:
Love

Plant Energy:
Walnut for Compassion

Crystal Power:
Green Tourmaline for Balance and Harmony

OCTOBER GETS ITS NAME FROM THE ROMAN WORD *OCTO*, MEANING "EIGHT," FROM WHEN IT WAS ORIGINALLY THE EIGHTH MONTH OF THE YEAR. OCTOBER IS BEST KNOWN FOR HALLOWEEN, THE LAST NIGHT OF THE MONTH, WHICH IS CELEBRATED WORLDWIDE AS A TIME WHEN WITCHES, SPOOKY THINGS, AND SPIRITS ROAM. IN THE NORTHERN HEMISPHERE, THE DAYS ARE MUCH SHORTER AND LEAVES FALL. IN THE SOUTHERN HEMISPHERE, SPRING HAS TRULY ARRIVED WITH THE EMPOWERING WARMTH OF THE SUN.

The first three weeks of October are energized by the sun moving through the zodiac sign of Libra, still concerned with balance, harmony, and good relationships. This is an excellent energy for casting spells to evoke warmth and friendship, making up with loved ones, and generally stirring new romance into your life. All spells cast during this month benefit from adding a rose quartz crystal to your spell ingredients, to maximize the gift of harmony and true love in your quest for happiness.

As the sun moves across the cusp of Scorpio around the 22nd, the energy changes to the element of Water. Emotions and feelings are now highlighted. This is the perfect time to work spells concerned with passion, sexuality, and all things to do with intense desires. With the 31st comes Halloween, whose origins date back to the ancient Celtic festival of Samhain, which marked the end of harvest and the beginning of winter, a time of year associated with death. On that night, the ghosts or spirits of the dead returned to the earth and were invoked through various forms of divination to help the living.

In the northern hemisphere, the constellation Scorpius appears to crawl across the southern sky, close to the horizon. But in the southern hemisphere, it passes high in the sky. In Greek mythology the vain hunter, Orion, boasted to the goddess Artemis that he would kill every animal on the earth. Although Artemis was known as a hunter, she was also a protectress of nature, and so she sent a giant scorpion to destroy Orion. The pair battled, and the scorpion eventually killed Orion by the sting in its tail. Zeus, at the request of Artemis, made the scorpion a constellation in the heavens, as he did Orion, as a reminder for mortals to curb excessive arrogance, the curse of most relationships.

FEAST OF MEDITRINA

ENCHANTMENT TO SEDUCE

The first vintage of the Roman wine season was offered to Meditrina, the goddess of wine, to ensure its successful trade across the whole of the empire. But more bewitching celebrations were associated with her power.

High priestesses dissolved pearls in the precious wine for healing purposes, and just before sunset on the same day, legend tells of how Meditrina made an aphrodisiac from wine, cloves, and nutmeg. She offered it to the sun god, Sol, seducing him into taking her with him on his golden chariot as it raced toward the night sky. You too can harness Meditrina's seductive powers by taking one sip of her magic potion while you petition her help.

It is best to cast your spell in the evening just before sunset to harness the symbolic power of the union of Sol and Meditrina.

Make a small circle of twelve pebbles, stones, or quartz crystals on the floor, or outside where the sunset energy is more intense. These twelve stones represent the twelve constellations through which Sol travels at night.

WHAT YOU WILL NEED

12 pebbles, stones, or white quartz crystals

A metal cup or bowl (preferably gold- or silver-plate, pewter, or copper)

4 white candles

A handful of red rose petals

3 cloves

A glass of red wine or grape juice

Place the metal bowl or cup in the center of the circle and sit or kneel before the circle facing west, the direction of the setting sun.

Place and light the four white candles to the west, north, east, and south of the bowl, in that order, to invoke the energy of the elements Water, Earth, Air, and Fire, which rule these directions respectively.

Close your eyes and gently focus in your mind on the qualities or image of the one you want to seduce. Do this for approximately three minutes.

Take the rose petals, which represent desire, and the three cloves—three to symbolize love, harmony, and togetherness—and place them in the vessel.

Take one sip of wine (or grape juice) and pour the rest into your cup or bowl. As you do so, affirm to yourself:

"Bless me, Meditrina, burning true and gold With power to take Sol round the world Bless me with power to court and woo And take what's mine both right and true."

Let the candles burn on while you focus again for three minutes on the one you want to seduce. Now blow the candles out. Thank Meditrina for her blessing and leave your enchantment in place overnight.

For the following week, you will be able to seduce anyone you choose.

CHONGYANG FESTIVAL

SPELL TO BIND A RELATIONSHIP

In the Far East, the ninth day of the ninth lunar month is known as the traditional Chongyang festival, or Double Ninth Festival. Because the lunar calendar is very different from the Gregorian calendar we use in the West, the actual date will change every year, so this spell can be activated at any time during the first three weeks of October.

 n the ancient Taoist magical text known as the I *Ching*, or *The Book of Changes*, the number 9 symbolized yang, which is potent masculine energy. *Chong* in Chinese means "double," or the number 2, and represents yin, receptive feminine energy. So the Chongyang festival celebrates the union of opposites. By drawing on the combined power of feminine yin energy and male yang energy in this spell, any long-term love relationship will be blessed and harmonized. The rings in this spell symbolize this power: silver to represent yin (feminine) and gold to represent yang (masculine).

WHAT YOU WILL NEED

2 rings (1 silver colored, 1 gold colored. However, real gold and silver are imbued with divine power and will maximize the power of the spell.)

Silken thread or ribbon

A pouch or bag made of silk or cotton

A small box with a lid or an envelope

1 white candle

1 red candle

In more recent times, *Chongyang* was pronounced the same as a Chinese word that means "forever," so the festival became associated with a perfect and auspicious time for binding relationships "forever." This spell works because of the power of numbers and their magical associations. Performing it in this auspicious month ensures a happy marriage or committed love partnership.

Tie the rings together with a silken thread or ribbon. Natural fabrics, such as gold and silver, are further imbued with divine energy.

Place the rings on your window ledge for three nights to amplify the power threefold by the light of the moon. Even if you can't see the moon, it is still there, working its magic.

Next, place your moon-enriched rings into the pouch or bag and place it under your pillow for four nights. Remove the next morning and carry the pouch with you wherever you go for five days.

Remove the rings from the pouch and place on the window ledge for six more days.

On the seventh day, carry it with you again until the ninth day.

On the ninth day, take the rings out of the pouch and seal them in a box or envelope. Place this in a drawer or special place forever.

On the tenth day, light the two candles—white for purity, red for passion—and affirm the following as you close your eyes:

"We are bound together forever, each in the other, as yin and yang are one."

From now on, you will be in harmony with your beloved, and they with you.

October 20

SUN MOVES INTO SCORPIO

AN ENCHANTMENT TO MAKE A DECISION

As the sun moves into Scorpio, Water energy brings flowing thoughts, and like the changing waves and tides of the sea, there is potential in every dream if you go with the flow. This spell draws on the power of the element Water, which in witchcraft is associated with the direction west.

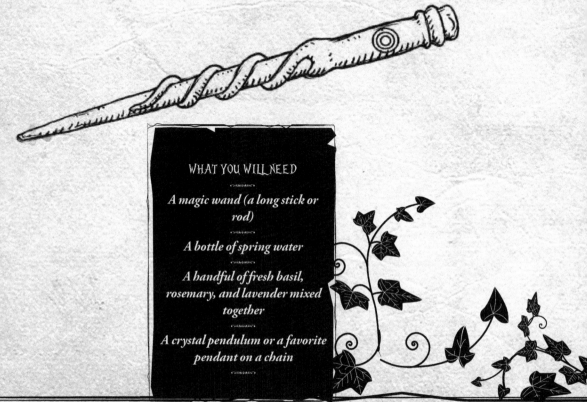

WHAT YOU WILL NEED

A magic wand (a long stick or rod)

A bottle of spring water

A handful of fresh basil, rosemary, and lavender mixed together

A crystal pendulum or a favorite pendant on a chain

ind a quiet space outside, perhaps your garden, a park, or the countryside. Stand facing west and draw an imaginary magic circle around you with your wand in a clockwise direction (see page 15).

Next, you are going to consecrate the west with your water and herbs. Sprinkle some water to the west of you and say,

"To the Waters of the West, I bless and honor your decision-making power."

Now sprinkle some of the mixed herbs in the same place.

Take up your crystal pendulum and concentrate on the decision you want to make. It may be very simple, such as a choice between jobs, partners, or moving away from home. But whatever the question, phrase it so there are only two possible answers, *yes* or *no*. Keep saying your question over and over in your mind, then stand above the consecrated ground where you sprinkled the water and herbs and hold the pendulum steady between your finger and thumb. Close your eyes and keep thinking about this question. The pendulum will start to swing of its own accord: If it swings perpendicularly or horizontally, the answer is no; if it swings around in a circle, whether clockwise or counterclockwise, the answer is yes.

The decision has been made for you by the solar energy of the west. However, if you don't agree and truly believe that the decision is not right for you, the magic has forced you to trust your deeper instincts and know in your heart what is truly right.

EOS EVE

SPELL TO BREAK AN INFATUATION

Eos was the Greek goddess of the dawn, cursed by Aphrodite to eternally fall in love with mortals. To the ancient Greeks, her rosy fingers represented the pink clouds of sunrise. But some sources believe she originated from a cult of ancient Egyptian witches who, when performing spells, stained their fingers red as blood, as a symbol of the life force. Eos represents the universal energy that flows through all things. As she rises every morning, she hopes one day that by helping others, her own curse will be broken.

 o break an infatuation, either yours or someone else's for you, you need to draw on the power of Eos and her life force.

Go for a walk, preferably alone, as early in the day and as near to sunrise as you can to draw on the full power of Eos. It can be in the garden, park, beach, or countryside, but make sure it's a safe environment.

As you walk, step slowly and look at the ground beneath you. When you see a small stone, pebble, shell, or any natural object, pick up any that appeal to you until you have seven stones. (The number seven connects us to magical or divine forces.) They should be small enough so you can carry them with you in your pocket or a small bag.

WHAT YOU WILL NEED

You

Each time you pick up a stone, hold it and feel its natural power permeating your skin, filling you with inspiration and spiritual power.

When you have seven stones, sit down in a comfortable place and put the stones in your lap. Close your eyes and concentrate on the person you want to banish from your life, but without intending them any harm.

As you repeat the enchantment below, remove one stone from your lap and throw it as far away from you as possible. Say,

"Eos, release me from the infatuation by tomorrow's dawn."

Then take a second stone, throw it far from you in any direction, and say,

"Eos, release me from the infatuation by the second dawn."

With the third stone, say,

"Eos, release me from the infatuation by the third dawn."

Continue in this way until you have thrown all seven stones from your lap and you have counted each throw as another dawn.

When you have finished, put your hands together in prayer and thank Eos for helping to release you from your love addiction.

Within seven dawns, this spell will work its magic and either you or someone else will no longer be bound by infatuation.

October 29

EOS DAY

TO STIR LOVE IN SOMEONE'S HEART

This spell also uses the power of Eos,
but this time to stir love in someone's heart.

 et up the candles in a large triangle on your altar or table with the red one, representing desire and love's potency, at the apex of the triangle. Make sure you have room to sit at the table, so you are almost between the two white candles, which represent purity.

Place the bowl of water in the middle of the triangle and light the incense to the east side of the triangle, to conjure up the power of Eos and the rising sun. Then light the candles.

WHAT YOU WILL NEED

1 red candle

2 white candles

A bowl of water

Sweet incense such as rose or vanilla

1 stemmed rose

With the stem of the rose, stir the bowl of water in a counterclockwise direction and imagine you are stirring love in your chosen suitor's heart.

Once the water is spinning around, pluck a petal from the rose and drop it into the water.

As you drop each petal, say the following enchantment so that a specific quality of your heart's desire is charged with love. For example,

"Empower his/her sense of humor with love."

"Empower his/her courage with love."

"Empower his/her kindness with love."

And so on. Continue to drop in petals for each characteristic you picture your love to have.

If the water stops spinning before you have finished describing the qualities, take the rose stem and stir it again until you have listed all the qualities you love about that person.

When the water stops spinning, the person you described will fall in love with you.

HALLOWEEN

ARIADNE'S SPELL TO SEDUCE

In the ancient palaces of Minoan Crete, high priestesses enchanted wealthy traders and seafarers using their feminine wiles, aphrodisiacs, and white magic. They worshipped the serpent goddess, who was also protectress, sorceress, and destroyer of evil. The Minoans traded extensively in their prize spice, saffron, and the stranger was enchanted into their serpent goddess—worshipping culture. It is believed that Ariadne, notorious for giving the hero Theseus a thread to find his way out of the labyrinth, was the original serpent goddess who guarded the secret of saffron magic. This love spell was used by priestesses whenever a rich stranger feasted in the palace at Knossos. According to legend, if any stranger appeared on the day of the year devoted to the ghosts of the ancestors (the day we know as Halloween), he would be brought to the palace of the serpent goddess to prove to her he was not a ghost, but a virile man!

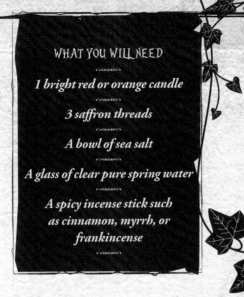

WHAT YOU WILL NEED

1 bright red or orange candle

3 saffron threads

A bowl of sea salt

A glass of clear pure spring water

A spicy incense stick such as cinnamon, myrrh, or frankincense

Place the candle on a table or on your special altar and place the saffron, salt, and water beside it. Light the candle, and as you do so, say,

"Oh, lady Ariadne, give me the power to seduce and the reward of my desire."

Now light the incense and let it burn until it is smoking.

Sprinkle the sea salt around the candle, and as you do so, say,

"Bring me my heart's desire, Oh sacred Earth."

Next, pass your hand in the air around the candle and say,

"Bring me my heart's desire, Oh sacred Fire."

Next, pass your hand through the smoke of the incense and say,

"Bring me my heart's desire, Oh sacred Air."

Drop the saffron into the water and say,

"Bring me my heart's desire, Oh sacred Water."

Next, touch the surface of the water and say the following:

"Oh, Ariadne, let desire be mine And with this spell, desire be theirs For me alone, but none to bind."

Now place your finger through the incense smoke and repeat the words of the spell again.

To release the energy, say,

"Ariadne, thank you for bringing me desire, seductive skills, and new love to my door. So mote it be."

Finally, snuff out the candle and incense, remove the threads of saffron from the water, and lay them on your altar. When dry, carefully place them in an envelope and keep them in a safe place to activate your seductive powers for the next three months.

NEW MOON SPELL

AN ENCHANTMENT TO ATTRACT ABUNDANCE TO YOU

This simple enchantment to perform on the evening of a new moon aligns you with the universe so that you can begin to attract good things into your life, whether new love, new job, new pleasure, or abundance.

 it before your altar or table and hold the white quartz crystal between both your hands. Stay still for a while and concentrate on its vibrational universal energy charging you with light and love.

Now say the following spell:

"I am of earth, sun, moon, and stars.
I am of Jupiter, Venus, and Mars.
I am of spirits and phantom faces.
Of unknown worlds and far distant places.
I am of prophets, magi, and rainbows,
Of gold, copper, silver, and all that doth flow.
I am a child of the universe, divine, wild, and true.
And all goodness I give, will come back to me too."

Place the quartz crystal on the table and leave for one lunar cycle for the magic to work and bring you the things you seek.

WHAT YOU WILL NEED

A white quartz crystal

FULL MOON SPELL

AN ENCHANTMENT TO ATTRACT GOOD BUSINESS CONTACTS

By working with the power of the magical talisman Populus (page 16), you can attract both public attention and beneficial people to ensure good business.

 ust after a new moon, draw or paint the symbol of Populus on a piece of paper and draw a circle around it. This is to contain the energy that flows between the two parallel lines. If you want to make people stop and notice you, you must contain their energy in this corresponding way.

Fold the paper eight times (the number that activates corporate power and big business) and write on the last folded side, "with blessings to all." Leave this paper in a closed drawer.

Bury the eight small pieces of bloodstone in the ground, as deep as two inches if possible, in the same pattern as Populus. This ritual of burying crystals or gems taps into the natural magic of the earth, and bloodstones promote both courage and strength.

If you can't bury them, place them in the same pattern in a covered box and place somewhere where they won't be disturbed. Again, whether buried or placed in a box, surround the two lines with a circle made of a piece of twine or cord.

After one week, remove one stone and carry it with you in your pocket or pouch until the next waxing moon; this will charge the stone with your personal charisma. At the full moon, return it to the remaining seven.

Keep safe both paper sigil and bloodstone symbols in their secret place for as long as you require. Soon you will be surrounded by people who can work their own personal magic for you, too.

WHAT YOU WILL NEED

A piece of paper and a pen or paint

8 small pieces of bloodstone

A covered box (optional)

Twine or cord

Chapter 12

NOVEMBER

Spells and Enchantments for Charisma and Passion

Theme:
Adventure

Plant Energy:
Yellow Chrysanthemum for Laughter

Crystal Power:
Citrine for Sparkling Communication

AS THE NORTHERN HEMISPHERE ENTERS THE WINTER SEASON,
THE SOUTHERN HEMISPHERE'S SUMMER IS NOT FAR AROUND THE
CORNER. THE COMING WINTER IS A TIME FOR USING CHARMS
FOR PROTECTION, CRAFTING SPELLS TO SEE YOU THROUGH THE
DEPTHS OF WINTER AND GIVE YOU THE OPTIMISM AND ENERGY
TO PLAN AHEAD FOR THE NEXT CALENDAR YEAR. AS ONE POET
WROTE, "IF WINTER COMES, CAN SPRING BE FAR BEHIND?"

Whatever the weather, there is always a sense of something changing, as the cycles of the sun and moon weave their tapestry throughout the year. With All Saints' Day and All Souls' Day marking the beginning of the month, November was named from the word *novo*, as it was originally the ninth month of the old Roman calendar. Throughout the world, many celebrations for the spirits of our ancestors are held in the first few days, such as the Day of the Dead in Mexico and the pagan festival of Hallowmas, as it was called in Shakespearean times.

For the first few weeks of the month, the sun continues to move through passionate Scorpio, but around the 22nd, it crosses the cusp of fire sign Sagittarius. While the sun is in this outgoing fire sign, it's time to show your true desires, work enchantments for romance and charismatic love, and prove that you are as adventurous in love and work as the renowned fiery people born under this sign (such as the novelist Jonathan Swift and film director Steven Spielberg).

The Babylonians identified the constellation of Sagittarius with the god Nergal, a strange, centaur-like creature firing an arrow from a bow. The ancient Greeks adopted the centaur archetype, but there are many myths about who the archer actually was. Some identify Sagittarius as the centaur Chiron, the wounded healer, but Chiron is represented by the constellation Centaurus. Another tradition suggests the archer not as a centaur but the satyr Crotus, son of Pan, whom the Greeks credited with the invention of archery. According to myth, Crotus often went hunting on horseback and lived among the Muses. He requested that Zeus place him in the sky, where he could be seen demonstrating his talents.

Sagittarius energy is about seeing great potentials and understanding cosmic wisdom and the "bigger picture" rather than only sifting through the details. This is a time when you don't need "evidence"—only experience—to understand how, by doing spell work, you can harness the power of the divine that flows through everything, including yourself.

November 1

HALLOWMAS

SPELL TO EMPOWER YOU WITH PASSION

The pagan celebration of souls, spirits, and ancestors, which started last night on Halloween, continues today. Aphrodite was also celebrated for her ability to bring pleasure to those who gave thanks to their ancestors and the gods. This Aphrodite love spell will bring passion into your life, whatever the weather.

 n your table or altar, lay out three circles of candles. Start with the white candles in the middle, then a ring of pink, and then red candles on the outer circle. Light all fifteen candles, one ring at a time, starting from the inside white ones.

Now say the following:

"By the power of
Aphrodite,
Bless my ritual with
passion
Bless my body with desire
My lover's with more
Both entwined in love
Let this kiss be the one
That sets us on fire
So mote it be."

WHAT YOU WILL NEED

5 white candles

5 pink candles

5 red candles

A conch or other seashell

A silk scarf (preferably red)

A piece of red yarn or ribbon

Now take up the shell and give it one kiss. Then say,

"By this kiss,
I bring Aphrodite's power
to this spell
To wash the oceans of her
love over me
To bring me passion's fire
And by this spell, so mote
it be."

Place the shell in the silk scarf and tie it up with red yarn or ribbon. Set the charm in the center of the inner candle circle without burning your hand!

Above the flames of the candles, quickly move your hand through the air in a spiraling circle moving your hand outward.

As you do, say the charm:

"By this shell,
I call on Aphrodite
To bring me all the desire
I need
So mote it be."

Once the candles have burned halfway down, blow them out, remove the silk scarf and shell, and place them under your mattress or pillow to generate true passion in your love life.

November 1-20
DIWALI

AN ENCHANTMENT FOR REVIVAL AND EMPOWERMENT

From the middle of October through the end November, depending on the lunar calendar, Hindus gather at temples throughout India to celebrate a festival of lights and the start of the Hindu new year. The festival is celebrated by offering the goddess Dharani her magical herb, basil, to ensure happiness in the future. The planetary positions in the heavens are also important signs on the day and are said to generate success for those who merit it. You can perform this spell at any time between the dates given above to ensure you are within range of the lunar calendar's specific energy.

This spell is for utter empowerment in one's own world and for shaking off the past. It is also to bring to life stagnant projects or things that you believed were ruined but can now be revived.

Before you perform this spell, take a ritual bath or shower with the perfumed oils to purge your body, mind, and soul of negativity.

WHAT YOU WILL NEED

Rosewater, jasmine, and sandalwood essential oils or perfumes

7 basil leaves

After your ritual, take the seven basil leaves and place them on a table in a circle as an offering to Dharani.

Next, call upon the energy of the planets in the following way: Each time you call up a planet, take one of the basil leaves to represent the planet and place it outside of the circumference of the circle.

"I call on Mercury, the planet of wisdom, to help me transform my beliefs.
I call on Venus, the planet of love, to help me with acceptance.
I call on Mars, the planet of initiative, to give me the drive to act.
I call on Jupiter, the planet of opportunity, to give me the courage to transform.
I call on Saturn, the planet of preservation, to keep me on my path.
I call on the moon, the planet of dreams, to make my wishes come true.
I call on the sun, the planet of success, to fulfill my goals."

You will now have a bigger circle of leaves. Take one leaf, any one that you like the look of, and eat it. This will invoke Dharani's energy and align you with the planetary energy of the day.

Finally, give thanks to Dharani, and very soon you will be able to transform your world.

November 22

SUN MOVES INTO SAGITTARIUS

ENFLAME A RELATIONSHIP CHARM

This spell is especially suited to when you have just begun a new relationship and want to make it sparkle with flirtatious fun and steamy sex. Fortuna was the goddess of luck and fate in Roman mythology. She turned the wheel of destiny, which decided whether you were to have good or bad luck. She was said to have enchanted Jupiter and taken all his luck for herself, then flew to the constellation of Sagittarius to be protected by Crotus, the hunter satyr, escaping Jupiter's vengeful lightning bolts. As the sun moves into Sagittarius around this day, invoke both Fortuna's and Jupiter's luck to empower you with passion.

WHAT YOU WILL NEED

A piece of paper and a pen

An envelope

1 piece of turquoise

1 piece of aquamarine

1 piece of calcite

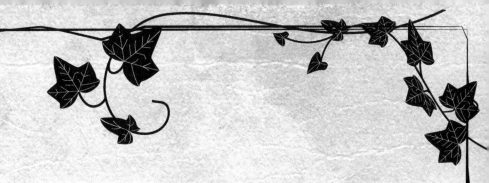

 his enchantment uses the magical symbol known as Laetitia, the Latin for "joy," to harness the power of Fortuna and her ability to bring you "joyful relating."

First, draw the Laetitia symbol (see page 16) on the piece of paper and write your name above the top of the symbol, plus your lover's name alongside your name.

Now beneath the symbol write the following:

"Oh, bountiful Fortuna, bless happiness with joy."

Next, fold the paper seven times and put it in an envelope. Keep it in a personal place, such as under your pillow, for seven nights to maximize the magic of luck and to invoke the power of Fortuna into your life.

On the seventh day, remove the paper and with the three crystals, place it in a window or on a table where they won't be disturbed. Turquoise opens you to the endless possibilities of joy in your love life, aquamarine gives you the courage to ask for your sexual needs to be met, and calcite helps you find joint pleasure in the simplest things. Make sure the point of the Laetitia symbol points to the west to attract positive happy energy into your life, and leave for another seven days for the magic to begin to work.

November 27

DAY OF FRIGGA

A VITALITY CHARM

Frigga was the consort of the mythical Norse god Odin, and she represents feminine power and outer beauty. She was known to carry a box of secret potions that turned ugly mortals into beautiful nymphs. With Frigga's magic vitality box, you can contain, invoke, capture, and exude all forms of seductive charms. Frigga was known as the beloved lady, her name possibly rooted in the ancient Sanskrit word *priya*, meaning "beloved." This charm means you can love yourself at all times, and it is the magical key to being vitalized.

 ake a piece of paper and write a list of all the qualities you aspire to, or what would make you feel beautiful, loved, or just good to be you.

Next, on the lid of the box, draw a triple moon symbol (see page 191) to represent Frigga's powers. Inside your paper wish list, place the photo of yourself, the white quartz, the twigs, and the acorn or oak leaf. Place the rose petals on top of the photo and close the lid.

WHAT YOU WILL NEED

A piece of paper and a pen

A small shallow box with a lid, such as a shoe box

A photo of yourself you truly like

1 white quartz crystal

Twigs of wood (preferably hazel or hawthorn)

1 acorn or oak leaf (or the image of one)

5 rose petals

As you do so, say,

"Oh, goddess Frigga,
Please bless this box of twigs
With beauty pure indeed
So I can be the best of myself
For all that I shall need."

Now place the box in a secret place, drawer, or under your bed. Whenever you want to draw on Frigga's beauty for yourself, or feel good to be you, take out the box and repeat the following words:

The triple moon symbol, also known as the triple goddess symbol.

"The dreams that lie within the earth awaken now.
The beauty in me will awaken now.
The stars await as so do I.
Grow true, grow strong, toward the sky."

Each time you open the box, take out the white quartz crystal, hold it in your hand, and repeat the spell above to maximize and embrace Frigga's beneficial help. You will be revitalized and ready for every opportunity or challenge that comes your way.

November 30
THE NIGHT OF TRIVIA

AN ENCHANTMENT TO MANIFEST SUCCESSFUL NEW VENTURES

The Roman goddess Trivia, equivalent to the Greek goddess Hecate, ruled over magic, sorcery, witchcraft, and divination. On the evening of the 30th, Romans would leave offerings to Trivia at their nearest crossroads in the hope that she would transmit good news about their future via oracular priestesses in her temple who told futures by divining patterns found in candle wax. By invoking Trivia's power, you can successfully get started with any new ventures in the next few months.

 lace the rose hips, nettle leaves, and sprigs of rosemary in the bowl of water. Bind together the two red candles (the color of desire) with the raffia (representing the manifest world). Stand the two candles in the bowl of water and light them. Now sit back and concentrate on the new business or wealth opportunity you are hoping for. If the wax doesn't drip easily, then hold the candles at an angle above the water.

WHAT YOU WILL NEED

3 rose hips (or rose hip tea)

3 nettle leaves (or nettle tea)

3 sprigs of rosemary

A bowl of ice-cold water

2 red candles

Raffia

Watch the patterns of wax forming in the water, just until you are ready to stop. You will know when you are ready; it is an inner gut feeling.

Now say,

"Come hither, Trivia,
Come now to the crossroads of choice
Come, having one mind with me
Draw near, and bestow grace upon my desire."

Gaze at the wax patterns until one catches your eye or stands out from the others and take it from the water. It may be attached to bigger patterns, so break the wax from the rest of the shapes and place it on the table, doing so carefully.

To manifest your desires, hold the wax shape in the palm of your hand and say the following spell:

"With Trivia's help good fortune comes.
With luck's desire and fire's truth
My flame of light has just begun."

Blow out the candles, relax, and within a few weeks you will begin to see new ventures and opportunities that will bring you success.

NEW MOON SPELL

A CHARM TO KEEP A LOVER FROM STRAYING

Sometimes we believe our love will leave us, but this spell, without doing any harm to your beloved, will activate his or her desire to stay put. You must do this spell only on the day after the new moon.

 raw a pentagram (page 15) on the paper and then in each of the five star points, write your name. In the center, write your lover's name.

Wrap the paper around the basil and amber and place all the ingredients into a pouch. Take it to a river, stream, lake, or pond (or use a bowl of spring water, if you can't).

Dip the pouch into the water, without letting go, and say the charm,

Take the pouch out of the water and now bury it somewhere secret and safe. Leave it there until you know, deep in your heart, that your love will be true to you forever.

"Thank you, goddess of the moon,
Fulfill my desire and let it be.
Direct his/her love only to me.
This is my will, so mote it be."

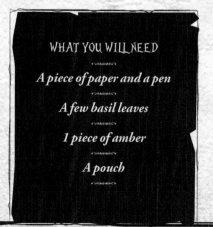

WHAT YOU WILL NEED

A piece of paper and a pen

A few basil leaves

1 piece of amber

A pouch

FULL MOON SPELL

A SPELL FOR BANISHING BAD ENERGY

Just after the full moon, use this spell to get rid of any unwanted energy in your life. This ancient magic square was once used to ward off all manner of evil. It will enable you to get rid of all that is unwanted in your life and help bring you all that you want to manifest.

 n the paper, write down this magic word square:

SATOR
AREPO
TENET
OPERA
ROTAS

Place a candle on the first letter of each line of the square from top to bottom and say the magic words,

"Sator, Arepo, Tenet, Opera, Rotas,
By the power of words all bad be gone.
By the power of words all wrongs be gone.
By the power of words all negativity be gone.
So mote it be."

Move the candles now to the last letter at the end of each line and finally light them. Now say the magic charm again. and sit for a few moments gazing into the candle flames before you blow them out. All negativity will be gone.

WHAT YOU WILL NEED

A piece of paper

A pen

5 red candles

SPELL TO MANIFEST NEW ROMANCE

The ancient Egyptian sky goddess, Nut, spread her star-spangled belly across the earth at night to protect all who worshipped her. When the sun god, Ra, was trapped in the earth and couldn't ride his chariot across the sky anymore, Nut turned into a huge cow that lifted him up to heaven so he could become the sun again. Nut was so exhausted that four gods rushed to her aid and later became the four winds, north, south, east, and west. This wind magic spell honors Nut and will also help you to whip up new romance or get someone to blow a gale of kisses in your direction.

WHAT YOU WILL NEED

*9 white candles and
9 red candles*

9 crushed rose petals

9 cinnamon sticks

A small bowl

Musk incense

A handful of earth

1 feather or bubbles

Water

ight the nine white candles (nine is Nut's number) and say,

"West Wind, bring new love to me.
East Wind, bring Nut's grace to me.
North Wind, let love come to me.
South Wind, send romance to me."

Light the nine red candles and call on Nut again: *"Nut, I call on you to bring his/her love for me to see."*

Then take the nine red rose petals and the nine cinnamon sticks and crush them up in a small bowl with your fingers. As you do so, say the following nine times:

"Thank you, Nut, for sending the winds to blow me new love."

Now go outside and, facing south, light the stick of musk incense and for a few seconds hold it toward the south. This will ignite a stranger's passion. To the north, throw a handful of soil into the wind to manifest a lover's presence. To the east, toss a feather or blow bubbles into the wind for rapid results. And finally, to the west, sprinkle water into the wind for emotional happiness. If it is not windy, don't worry; any air that is circulating will pick up on your enchantment for the winds.

Finally, take the crushed cinnamon sticks and rose petals and bury them in a sacred or secret place. In a few weeks, your new love will be by your side.

Chapter 13

DECEMBER

Spells and Enchantments for an Inspirational Future

Theme:
Integrity and Purpose

Plant Energy:
Holly for Victory

Crystal Power:
Turquoise for Happiness

FROM THE ROMAN WORD *DECEM*, MEANING "TEN," DECEMBER WAS ORIGINALLY THE TENTH MONTH OF THE PRE-JULIAN CALENDAR. THIS IS ONE OF THE MOST IMPORTANT TIMES IN THE YEAR, WHEN THE WINTER SOLSTICE IN THE NORTHERN HEMISPHERE MARKS A HUGE TURNING POINT. FROM THE 22ND ONWARD, THE DAYS GRADUALLY LENGTHEN, AND EVEN IN THE DEPTHS OF A BLEAK, COLD WINTER, SPRING SEEMS NOT SO FAR AWAY. IN THE SOUTHERN HEMISPHERE, THE SUMMER SOLSTICE MARKS THE HIGHLIGHT OF THE SUMMER, AND AGAIN A MOVE AND CHANGE OF THE SUN'S ENERGY AND POWER.

 special month in Christian traditions, December was also important in ancient Rome, where the Saturnalia, a big feast lasting several days from around the 17th through the 22nd, was a license to indulge in anything from gambling to group orgies. Another festival was the pagan Yule feast, which celebrated the changing solar cycle. Magic spells were concerned with purification, banishing the blues, increasing vitality, and inspiring ideas and plans for new life directions.

For the first three weeks of December, the sun continues to move through the fiery flames of the zodiac sign of Sagittarius. This is optimistic energy, and spells can be maximized by adding pieces of turquoise (Sagittarius crystal) to your magic ingredients. As the sun moves into Capricorn around the 21st, we move from the element Fire to that of Earth. Ruled by the planet Saturn, this energy is considered to be earthy, materialistic, and cautious. People born under Capricorn are often considered quietly ambitious. Innately aware of the rhythms and cycles of life, they know when to make crucial decisions to manifest their dreams.

In the last week of December, this is a time not only for celebrations, whatever your belief system, but a time to cast spells to restore order in your world. It's also a time to look to the future and see that with dedicated spell work to enhance your life, you can look forward to another successful year, where magic is working for you and those you love.

December 4

THE FEAST OF BONA DEA

LIFE DIRECTION ENCHANTMENT

Bona Dea was an earth goddess in Roman mythology who was associated with fertility and abundance. As mother earth, she was invoked or worshipped during important rites of passage, such as birth, entering adulthood, and death. Because she represents the cycle of change and growth, you can invoke her powers to change your life direction in the way you want.

 irst, place one piece of topaz in a drawer in the room where you spend most of your time—for example, your kitchen or a study—and this will encourage lucrative energy for business success.

Lay out the remaining five pieces of topaz in the shape of the points of a pentagram (page 15) anywhere in your home where they won't be disturbed.

WHAT YOU WILL NEED

6 small pieces of mystic topaz

2 green candles

1 white candle

1 red candle

1 yellow candle

For five evenings in a row, do the following:

On the first night, light one green candle to honor Bona Dea and place it beside the point at the top of the pentagram. Let it burn for ten minutes while you gaze at the pentagram and repeat these words,

> "Thank you, Bona Dea, for your power. With this help, my life will flower."

Blow out the candle and leave it in its place.

On the second night, light one white candle and place it beside the next point of the star in a clockwise direction. Keep this lit for 10 minutes while you concentrate on the symbol, repeat the spell above, then blow the candle out and leave it beside the pentagram point.

On the third night, light a red candle beside the third star point and again let it burn for ten minutes, then repeat the spell and so on.

On the fourth night, repeat again with a yellow candle.

On the fifth night, repeat with the second green candle and this time say,

> "Thank you, Bona Dea, for what will come. Abundance draws powers from the Sun And with this topaz, Five is One For what is turned, can't be undone."

Place the five stones in a pouch, keep it in a safe place, and then remove the candles.

From now on you can choose your own life direction and know it is the right one to bring you happiness and the things you truly desire.

GALUNGAN CEREMONY

A BANISHING SPELL TO HELP MANIFEST DREAMS

In Bali around this time of year, there is a week in which the gods and ancestors descend to earth and good triumphs over evil. Traditionally, the Balinese use magic healing and supplications to cleanse and protect themselves from bad spirits. They also honor Vac, the goddess of charms and talismans. According to legend, Vac's power is present in all words when she appears as the Goddess of Speech. Invoking her magic will help you banish negativity from your life.

WHAT YOU WILL NEED

A white sage smudging stick

A bunch of fresh flowers
(whatever is in season)

Sandalwood incense

A piece of paper and a pen

irst, do a simple spring cleaning of your home. This not only "cleanses" your home physically, but mentally and emotionally helps to declutter your mind, clearing the spiritual energy around you. Once you have literally cleaned up, take the bunch of sage and walk around every room of your home with the stick just smoldering. This will clear any remaining negative energy.

Next, place the flowers on your altar and say,

"Thank you, Vac, for your presence here.
In all I do, think, say, or fear
Please banish the bad and bring in the good
So that dreams be attained in the way that they should."

Next, light the incense to welcome Vac into your home, and at the table, write the following on your piece of paper in your best handwriting:

"Like Vac, I will myself announce and utter the words that gods and men alike shall welcome."

With Vac's blessing, these words will be truly magical for you.

Finally, place the paper in a safe place for the rest of the year. Now that your home and your world are safe and all negativity is banished, you can start to work on manifesting your dreams.

December 20

SUN IN CAPRICORN

STEPPING OVER OR CROSSING A BOUNDARY

As the sun moves into Capricorn, the elemental magical energy now changes from Fire to Earth. By invoking the power of the planet Saturn, the ruler of Capricorn, you can cross the cusp of your old life and move into a new one. This spell uses Saturn's power to help you step over the line, literally, and begin afresh. It will enable you to cross any boundary in that you can change your environment, status, job, or relationships with the energy of today, simply by crossing over a symbolic "high magic boundary" guarded by Saturn.

 ind a quiet place outside in the garden, countryside, or a park. Sit down on the ground in a comfortable spot and concentrate on the boundary you wish to cross, which will change your life. It may be a "physical" boundary, such as a career change, moving abroad, a financial opportunity, or a relationship change. Or it may be an emotional boundary, such as moving away from loss or rejection; giving up an obsession; or desiring to be calmer, more tolerant, more willing, less dependent, and more self-reliant. Whatever your personal boundary that needs to be crossed, accept it now and repeat to yourself the mantra of acceptance as you begin to perform this ritual:

"I accept I must cross this boundary. I accept the change that will transform me."

WHAT YOU WILL NEED

A 3-foot (90-cm) length of rope or twine (Or you can twist and knot together pieces of string, rope, or any fabric that you like.)

A very large stone or rock

A small cup of corn

A small cup of red wine

Once you seriously believe what you say to yourself, lay the rope out in a line and place the large stone, to represent Saturn, about halfway along. Take the small cup of corn and sprinkle it over the stone. Repeat your mantra of acceptance as you do so.

Then say, *"Thanks be, blessed Saturn of night and stars,*
To give me wisdom and your prayers.
My goodness let the world to see
My passion, fire, my talents be
To bring me happiness that's now due.
So thrice again I say to you
And thrice again, I say on high
To win gold wings to make this mine
This boundary crossed,
This blockage passed.
I now will move beyond your stone
And win the power of joy alone."

Now pour the wine over the stone and repeat your mantra of acceptance.

Now you are ready to cross the boundary. Take a deep breath and relax. Stand before the rope and take one step over it so that one foot is on one side and the other foot is on the other side. As you stand like this with one foot on either side of the rope just for one minute, repeat your acceptance mantra as many times as you can. Take your back foot off the ground and place it beside your other foot on the other side of the boundary.

You have now crossed the boundary, and the magic will begin to work as you step into the new you, the new world you have created for yourself, or simply a new beginning.

Now say,

"I have crossed the boundary
of transformation and I
am now ready to make the
change, so mote it be."

This final affirmation is the best magic you can give yourself, but like any of the magic spells here, utter belief in the powers you are invoking is essential for the spell to work!

WINTER SOLSTICE

SPELL TO BRING BENEFICIAL INFLUENCES ON YOUR TRAVELS

We all want to be able to leave, temporarily or otherwise, our family home at some point in our lives. It may seem as if we are "breaking vows" too. It may be because of unforeseen circumstances, the desire for a quest to find new adventure or take a golden opportunity, or just a need to explore the world before returning to our roots.

hatever the case, if you want to leave home, by invoking the protective powers of Ops, the earth goddess married to Saturn, you can make your change a positive one for as long as you want to be away. When Roman family members traveled for any reason, they often carried a small sheaf of corn (Ops's main attribute) for protection or placed it on the threshold of their home to ensure a safe return.

WHAT YOU WILL NEED

2 pieces of aquamarine

3 pieces of beryl

A small pouch

A small kitchen knife

1 white candle

Frankincense incense

First, sit quietly, relax, and concentrate on your destination. Take the pieces of aquamarine and beryl (both protective talismans when traveling) and place them in the pouch.

With the knife, carve into the side of the candle the name of the place you are going to visit.

Light the candle and the incense and pass the pouch back and forth seven times through the smoke of the incense to invoke the help of Ops. Concentrate on the candle flame. Now open the pouch, take out the five stones, and place them in a circle around the candle.

Say the following,

"Wherever I go in the East,
This heart of my home will never be least.
Wherever I go in the North,
There will always be time to again set forth.
Wherever I go in the South,
This heart of my home will be a safe path.
Wherever I go in the West,
From now on my travels will be for the best."

Thank Ops for her help and then take the five stones and place them back in the pouch. Carry them with you on your travels for protection and safe homecoming.

December 24

MODRANIHT

ENCHANTMENT TO AID CREATIVE THINKING

The Modraniht, or "Mothers Night," was a pagan festival celebrating the triad of mother goddesses known as the Matres. Their energy will enable you to get in touch with your imagination and put your creative "hat" on in any situation. This flowing magic will also mean you can persuade anyone to your ideas, thoughts, or plans for the future, and it is also a great spell if you are suffering from a temporary bout of writer's block.

WHAT YOU WILL NEED

3 white candles

A piece of paper and a pen

1 green leaf (or an image)

1 yellow flower (or an image)

1 blue flower (or an image)

A bowl of spring water

lace the candles in a triangle on your altar or table, light them, and sit quietly for a few moments to calm your mind.

Write down on the paper anything that bothers you, such as lack of creative thoughts, negative influences, and so on. Leave the paper beside the candles. Take up the green leaf and the yellow and blue flowers (or their images) in a bunch and hold them close to your "third eye" chakra—against the middle of your brow above your eyes—as you say the following:

"Blessed Matres, bring me magic charm
To move others without doing harm
Whereby the green, the yellow, and blue
Take not daggers, but speak only truth
So night and day, the stars and moon
Culminate in all that's done
And with this spell, so mote it be."

Place the flowers and leaf in the bowl of water and say,

"Thank you, Matres, for your help.
Please send all creative thoughts my way."

Pass your hands, with your palms down, in a clockwise circle over the bowl and repeat the above thanks twice more as you do so. Within a few days, your creative flow will be empowered for the coming new year and your future plans.

EIRENE'S HOUR

AN ENCHANTMENT FOR PEACE AND HAPPINESS

Eirene was the goddess of peace, depicted in art as a beautiful young woman carrying a cornucopia, a horn filled with abundant fruits, nuts, and seasonal flowers and herbs. She was one of the three Horai, the goddesses of the seasons and the keepers of the gates of heaven. The word hora means "the correct moment," and this is the perfect moment to call on Eirene to bring you a happy future.

WHAT YOU WILL NEED

A horn of plenty.(This can be a horn-shaped drinking vessel or bowl, or you can make a replica by twisting a conical shape out of stiff paper and then stapling the edges to keep it in shape.)

3 fruits (a pomegranate, a fig, an apple, or grapes are best)

Rose petals

1 sprig of lavender (or pinch of dried lavender)

A piece of paper and a pen

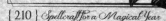

24

The symbol for Jupiter

 ecause Eirene also personified one of the Nine Hours of the day, which were classified between sunrise and sunset, perform this spell during her "hour," which falls between 1 p.m. and 2 p.m., to align with her correct moment.

At precisely 1 p.m., fill your horn with the various fruits and herbs. Place carefully on your altar or on a table as an offering to Eirene.

Next, on a piece of paper, draw the glyph for the sun (a circle with a dot in the center) on one side and the glyph for Jupiter on the other side (see this page). Fold it carefully four times and place it on your altar or sacred space next to the horn of plenty.

Leave your horn of plenty and the paper charm to Eirene until the clock strikes 2 p.m. and then remove it from the table or altar. Take the paper talisman and place it in a drawer in your desk or keep it with you in your handbag if you are traveling throughout the day, to ensure peace and happiness for the new year.

Now say,

"For peace and wealth, bring me thy skill,
Within this talisman luck instill
That I may fare successfully,
As I will, so mote it be."

NEW MOON SPELL

The patroness of weaving, Athena, was also the Greek goddess of wisdom, courage, inspiration, civilization, law and justice, just warfare, mathematics, strength, strategy, the arts, crafts, and skill! The owl was sacred to her, as was the olive tree, and she may have originated from an ancient Sumerian bird goddess depicted with talon feet and wings. This weaving spell calls on Athena's help to weave love and wisdom into your home and to bring peace and harmony.

The ingredients are all colors and fabrics associated with Athena's elements, Fire and Air.

First, lay out the white cloth on your altar, table, or somewhere you will be able to leave it for three days without the spell being disturbed.

Place the three red candles to the left of the cloth and the three yellow candles to the right.

WHAT YOU WILL NEED

A white cloth made of silk, cotton, or linen, about 2 feet (60 cm) long and 1 foot (30 cm) wide

3 red candles

3 yellow candles

3 red silk ribbons, about 2 feet (60 cm) long

3 yellow velvet ribbons, about 2 feet (60 cm) long

Take one red ribbon and two yellow ribbons, tie a knot at the end, braid them until you get to the end, and tie a second knot. Lay the braid along the length of the cloth, then do the same thing with the two red ribbons and the remaining yellow ribbon.

Now light the candles, and as you do so, say,

"I call on you, Athena,
to be my guide today
To help me weave blessing
and harmony
Upon my home,
always."

Next, take up the two woven braids, one in each hand, and hold them up in the air above the cloth (but take care not to let them get singed by the candles).

As you hold them, say,

"With woven ribbons my home is safe
With woven threads comes love and peace
With woven colors yellow and red
I now invoke Athena's grace
To make this home the perfect place."

Finally, blow out the candles, then place the braided ribbons back on the altar cloth for three days and three nights to bring Athena's harmonious influence to your home.

FULL MOON SPELL FOR GOOD BUSINESS

This charm is made up of a series of reinforcements, which will enable you to make your business even better. It will ensure that all those you meet are stunned by your talents and abilities.

WHAT YOU WILL NEED

1 piece of fire agate or ruby

1 large piece of fire agate

1 piece of aventurine

A piece of paper and a pen

1 piece of citrine

To encourage a dynamic business life, place a piece of fire agate or ruby under your pillow or bed.

To attract good contacts to you, put as large a piece of agate as will fit on a window ledge where there is maximum moonlight to enhance your vitality.

For vitalizing ideas, creative thinking, and brainstorming success, place a piece of aventurine in your office desk or by your computer.

Once all your crystals are in place, do the following:

On the evening of the full moon, to maximize the culminating power of the lunar cycle, draw a row of three pentagrams (page 15) on a piece of paper, then place the paper so that the top points of the pentagrams are facing east. On top of the middle pentagram, lay the piece of citrine (the crystal of business and communication success) to attract abundance.

Then every day for five days, take the citrine in your hands, focus hard for three minutes on what you really want most for a successful business, and place it back on the paper.

Each time, repeat the following spell:

"By citrine bright
By citrine true
My business world will be ensured
Success and progress, both fulfilled."

After five days, purify the citrine by washing it in clear spring water and then leave it on a window ledge where it can attract the moon's powers for three nights. Now that it is charged with the moon's magic, carry it with you wherever you go in a small pouch or your bag. This will increase your business success threefold and will draw important new contacts to you, as well as potential deals or new goals.

EPILOGUE

My Sorceress lives with the sun and the stars,
She sleeps by the falls of Venus and Mars
And her heart is drawn by the sway of the Moon
When whispers of love can beckon too soon.

Stern Saturn guides her to know her place
When the Winds of Chaos line energy's face,
And Jupiter holds her and kisses her now
As she trickles clear water on Neptune's brow.

For her head is turned by Mercurial charm,
And the eyes to her soul are peculiarly armed
With Uranian light that has seen Pluto's hell,
For who is she, but just a child of my spell?

ACKNOWLEDGMENTS

Thanks to everyone at Fair Winds Press for making this book
so beautiful; especially Jill Alexander for her personal magic, and
Jennifer Kushnier for her bewitching advice. I also want to thank my
agent, Chelsey Fox, for her eternal support, and my family for being
who they are and believing in the magic of the universe.

ABOUT THE AUTHOR

☙❧

Sarah Bartlett is the author of more than twenty psycho-spiritual non-fiction books, including the best-selling Tarot Bible. She has been astrologer for the London Evening Standard, Cosmopolitan, She, and Spirit and Destiny. She is also one of the founder members of www.theastrologyroom.com, where she provides both weekly content and a consultation service.

After studying for an art degree at Middlesex University in London, Sarah went on to become a consultant astrologer, first training at the Faculty of Astrological Studies in London, and then acquiring the diploma in psychological astrology at the Centre for Psychological Astrology, an in-depth, three-year professional training program that cross-fertilizes the fields of astrology, mythology and depth, and humanistic and transpersonal psychology.

Sarah currently contributes as astrologer to the Steve Wright in the Afternoon Show on BBC Radio 2 and divides her time between London and the South of France, where she teaches and practices the occult arts.

INDEX

CPSIA information can be obtained
at www.ICGtesting.com
Printed in the USA
FSOW03n2335141117
41043FS